SUITE
DEAL

SUITE DEAL

The Smart Landlord's Guide to Leasing Real Estate

ALICE DEVINE

LEARN
ASSOCIATES
— PUBLISHING —

LEARN
ASSOCIATES
— PUBLISHING —

Published by Learn Associates Publishing
Belmont, California
www.suitedealbook.com

Design: Paul Barrett
Editorial: Alexander Rigby, Valerie Paquin, Kari Somerton
Image credits: Halkin Mason Photography

ISBN (paperback): 978-1-7335307-0-5
ISBN (ebook): 978-1-7335307-1-2

Dedicated to William Wilson & Associates for its visionary leadership and quality real estate developments

CONTENTS

PREFACE

Commercial real estate is a go-go business that thrives on hip architecture, charismatic people, and the thrill of a deal. The process of learning how to acquire and retain quality tenants, however, resembles a glacier moving ever . . . so . . . slowly. Why? Perhaps because real estate's standard field training remains somewhat haphazard. Perhaps because its traditional culture limits access. Perhaps because leasing is part science, part art—precise business terms and intuitive skills. Perhaps—probably—because of all of the above.

As I started my career in real estate, I discovered that my contemporaries who had been hired in other industries benefited from robust training programs designed to expose them to the many facets of their chosen businesses. In contrast, my training was informal and largely dependent on the quality of my mentors, whom, as I came to understand, I was lucky to have had at all. A further complication was commercial real estate's notoriously "old-boy" atmosphere, which was entirely new territory for me. And acquiring the skills I needed to succeed as a property manager and leasing professional—both the analytical and people skills—took time. The beginning of my career was a baptism of fire that sometimes ended in a spectacular flameout of defaulting tenants and muddied lease terms.

Over the years, the companies for which I worked managed, bought, built, and renovated commercial properties. As landlords, we leased millions of square feet of office space and established close working relationships with quality tenants who became famously reluctant to leave our buildings. Through it all, I found I had a well-developed sense for leasing—an instinct, honed by experience, that told me a deal was ours to close, even in the early tour stages.

Why care about upping your leasing skills? Because effective leases add value to properties. Let's do some simple math. Suppose, for example, that you negotiate a mere 5 cents per square foot per month more in rent because you've read this book. That's 60 cents per square foot per year. In a 100,000 square foot building, the increased rental rate translates to $60,000 more in annual revenue. Capped at 6% (more about this in chapter 7), that additional rent has added $1,000,000 to the building's value! So leasing matters for a property's value . . . and it translates to one's professional worth.

This book is intended primarily for those in commercial real estate whose responsibilities include leasing (or some aspect of it), and will benefit property managers, asset managers, landlords, leasing agents, and brokers. Having said that, much of this leasing discussion will benefit those who work with multifamily properties as well. The book is divided into three main sections: preparing to lease space, structuring the lease deal, and closing the lease deal. The chapters mirror the extensive training program I have designed and taught to commercial property managers. My intent is to be practical and sequential, and to speak to the realities of leasing.

Of course, in real estate, daily life rarely follows the neat sequence of a book, so take a deep breath and appreciate this crazy business for its infinite variety. You might be thrust into a tour of vacant space your first day on the job. A tenant might ask you about renewing a lease as you stand waiting for coffee. You might—lucky you—inherit a property, and although there may be a leasing team in place, you'll want to understand how the market works. Your only certainty is that each day will be different from the last.

My grandfather once suggested, "Begin where the other person left off." Failing to listen to his advice, I undoubtedly retraced steps taken by others. This book gives you the opportunity to forge your own path with the benefit of others' experiences and knowledge. I have tried to write in such a way that regardless of what leasing challenge you may encounter, you will be able to turn to a chapter and obtain help toward a solution. If my experience is any guide, the more problems you are able to solve, the better you will become at what you do. Inside, you will find practical leasing advice and real-life stories (in italics) gathered over hundreds of transactions. (As a note, the words *landlord* and *owner* are used interchangeably in this book, as are the words *broker, agent,* and *salesperson.*)

Like most real estate documents, this one contains a disclaimer. This book is not intended to offer legal or accounting advice, but rather to serve only as a guide relevant to the daily tasks of leasing. For those subjects where legal or financial advice is required, you should seek the advice of professionals in those fields.

I'd love to hear from you about what works, what doesn't, and your own leasing experiences. Please visit my website, www.devinerealestateguide.com, for discussion, news, and relevant leasing topics. So hang on to your purses and wallets, and let's go.

PART I

Preparing to Lease Space

CHAPTER 1

Understand the Local Market

"I want to see everybody in their habitat."[1]
—*Sam Zell, founder, Equity International and real estate magnate*

GOAL: UNDERSTAND THE LOCAL REAL ESTATE MARKET IN ORDER TO POSITION A PROPERTY COMPETITIVELY

One afternoon, I received a telephone call and was hired to lease and manage a million square feet of commercial office space on the San Francisco Peninsula. Initially elated, I soon became concerned. Although a native San Franciscan, I knew little about the small towns south of the city and just north of Silicon Valley where this new portfolio was located. The area seemed an eclectic mix. One town boasted a card casino open twenty-four hours while the next town's tree-lined roads obscured mansions that housed CEOs and heirs to fortunes. Soon, office space featuring Ping-Pong tables for hoodie-clad techies would become fashionable. In the meantime, I needed to understand this marketplace. One of the first things I did was call the broker whose number was posted on a leasing sign at a large building in the area. Over the next three years, this broker helped me understand the market and, in the process, became a trusted friend.

It's said that commercial real estate professionals only care about the space within an hour's driving distance from their pillows. That quip underscores accurately the very local nature of real estate—for many, only the buildings within their competitive market affect their daily leasing lives. It follows that by focusing on your immediate real estate market and its competing buildings, you can position your own property for leasing success.

Learning about your local market allows you to succeed within it. Quantitatively, you must know and understand the features of the area, its inhabitants, properties, economics, culture, geography, and nuances.

In addition to knowledge of the quantifiable aspects of the local market, successful leasing requires a good understanding of people. An expert in human behavior, former CIA operative Henry A. Crumpton writes that "the heart of intelligence . . . is human espionage."[2] While you may aim to lease office space rather than provide national security, the importance of understanding people and what motivates their decisions applies equally to both.

How, then, do you gather the information you need in order to understand your market?

Learn from the Brokerage Community

READ BROKERAGE REPORTS

Online brokerage market reports can offer an expedient overview of real estate markets. Many real estate brokerages—especially national companies that often have extensive research staff—keep their fingers on the pulse of local markets by publishing regular blogs, online statistics, and market reports.

Market science, however, is inexact. Brokerages can report the same data differently by using their own definitions of neighborhoods, net rents, and square-footage absorption rates. While this lack of consistency can prove frustrating, when taken as a whole, the information should provide a good general overview of the marketplace. Take the reports for what they are—a broad brush of the local real estate landscape. (See appendix A for a list of firms that publish market research reports.)

Finding King Kong

Nearly every market has its "King Kong" of brokers, who may also write a blog or publish reports. These independent reports can have the added bonus of a more authentic voice, uncensored by a corporation's red pen. To find your local King Kong, contact the research staff of the three largest brokerage companies in your area and ask if any individual brokers publish such, and look for broker names posted on large buildings.

DEVELOP AND UTILIZE BROKER RELATIONSHIPS

Next, develop broker relationships to better understand a marketplace. As a starting point, choose several local brokers who represent buildings or tenants that you find similar to yours and ask how they feel your properties compare to others in the marketplace. If you get a sugar-coated response, talk to other brokers until you get more honest feedback. Remember that this is a time to listen, not to defend. When you get a broker's advice about improvements for your properties, you will have received valuable information, because most local tenants will likely share—or at the very least be influenced by—these same perspectives. Such feedback will allow you to develop a sense of what local brokers and tenants value, and enable you to create a better marketing plan.

ASK YOUR LOCAL BROKER FOR FEEDBACK

☐ How does my property compare to others in the marketplace?

☐ Which of my property's attributes are superior to those of other properties?

☐ Do you view any aspects of my property as detrimental?

☐ What, in your opinion, could be improved?

☐ What tends to be the most important decision factor for your clients? (See chapter 4 for more discussion about working with brokers.)

MEET BROKERAGE ANALYSTS

In addition to brokers, company analysts responsible for writing and publishing market reports can be a valuable resource. Unlike brokers, analysts—with a business card titled Market Research Analyst or something similar—can work far from the milieu of the private golf course, so buying them lunch or dinner can be a thoughtful gesture that encourages conversation. You will hear opinions about various landlords, evaluations of space in the market, and quite possibly, the current best—and worst—jokes.

CONVERSE ABOUT COMPARABLES

Economics 101 tells us markets are all about supply and demand, and that the truest test of correct pricing is what the market will bear. In commercial property leasing, signed leases—known as *comparables* or *comps*—reveal the value of a space according to the rent along with lease concessions (such as tenant improvements, rights to expand, etc.). The primary use of comps is to justify the offered terms of a lease as competitive and fair for the local marketplace. A complete comp generally contains all the economic terms (rent, square footage, term length, tenant improvements, etc.) of fully executed lease deals as well as other pertinent information, such as expansion or extension rights. The brokerage (and landlord) community tends to closely protect comps, using them to bolster their positions and volunteering only the information that doesn't weaken a negotiating stance. Effective leasing agents garner, guard, and use market information to their advantage.

How can a less experienced real estate professional accumulate a good bank of comps? By obtaining published comparables (via subscription and the other reports discussed above) and expanding them with information gleaned from your own industry connections. Although word-of-mouth information needs to be taken with a grain of salt, personal conversations allow for a certain freedom, often off the record. These discussions, however, still need to be cross-checked because they can be a mix of speculation and fact.

Once you have assembled all the data available on comparable deals in your area, you should have a good idea how your deal (or any deal) stacks up relative to the marketplace. The nature of these comparisons is such that while some spaces will stand out as direct competitors, others may be market indicators but will not share a one-to-one correspondence. Suppose, for example, that one space offers a view of the San Francisco Bay while another looks out over shrubs. How do you value each property's view as it relates to rent? Even professional appraisers struggle with quantifying certain subjective aspects of space. The idea, therefore, is to compile as large a group of comparables as possible to ascertain a range of justifiable rents. After that point, the success or failure of the transaction will likely boil down to a tenant's personal preference or, perhaps, some "softer" aspect (such as great property management service) that will tip the balance in your competitive leasing favor.

All the World's a Stage

Try role-playing to improve your information gathering. It takes practice to develop an informed yet easy conversational style that allows useful give and take. Overzealous information gathering can alienate others. So find a peer and practice exchanging the details of comparable lease terms.

Selecting the Right Tone

When seeking market information, many leasing agents use a reciprocal style; the more detailed and open the broker is with comparables, the more information you trade. Keeping the concept of *exchange* front and center allows you a balanced conversation in which you don't give away many details with scant information in return.

Choosing What Information to Trade

When you talk with brokers, appraisers, and other property managers, how do you know what comparable information to discuss? In terms of the information you receive, you are searching for the deal details on large tenants, or tenants who toured your property (but leased space at another building), or information on *any* portion of a deal. Because you keep a log of deal information, every bit of new data is valuable. Over time, the body of comparables you gather will probably become substantive, and you can ask for missing specifics to fill in the gaps.

When it comes to providing comparables, many real estate professionals prefer to trade information that already resides (more or less) in the public domain, because they do not want to release privileged details that may hurt their own negotiations. Which deals are public? Usually the ones that involved a broker, as the individual brokers and their employing brokerage houses certainly know the lease details. The more brokers involved—for example, a transaction that includes both a listing and a procuring broker—the more widespread the information. On the other hand, a lease renewal made directly between a landlord and an existing tenant (and without a representing broker) would be considered more private information. The best agents are conversant with all the public information and look for details or deals that have not been published. Evaluate the experience of the individual with whom you discuss deals—the information you trade will depend, to some extent, on the level or depth of that individual's knowledge. In many instances, you may be able to trade information about deals done at other properties, or deals already publicly discussed, and only as a last resort have to share any of your own private comparables. Remember that amplifying someone else's comps also counts as an information trade. For example, you can point out that one suite enjoys a panoramic view while another does not, which is likely reflected in the rent or another aspect of the lease. The more you understand your local marketplace, the better you become at discussing properties and lease transactions.

> *I remember a conversation with a local broker who complained that our building had a higher rental rate than the competitor across the street. I explained that our property was well constructed, with concrete floors and a steel frame, while the other building had a wood frame. The broker asked, "Who cares, since the floors are carpeted anyway?" I answered, "The tenant who walks across a squeaky wood-framed floor every time he crosses the office cares." Articulating the features of the space you lease allows you to call attention to its benefits and, ultimately, to justify the deal terms as you compete against other properties.*

Talking with Appraisers

Occasionally, appraisers will contact you to obtain comps, typically in preparation for a potential sale in the market. Because appraisers are usually working on a specific project, you can take a more transactional approach to information (as opposed to your long-term relationship building with the brokerage community). So, prior to giving away information, feel free to ask appraisers if they will send a copy of the market report they prepare or if they will exchange one or two comps. If the appraiser declines, you have every right not to provide any information at all, or only to offer comps already in the public domain.

KEEPING TRACK OF IT ALL

Whether you use a software program or go old school with a paper form, record information as you acquire it, even if it's just a portion of the deal. Then, fill in the gaps over time. For example, if you know about prospective tenants in the marketplace (most likely because they've toured your property), write their names on the comp sheet. If prospects don't sign a lease at your property, you can find out where they settled along with the transaction details, such as square footage, rent, term length, tenant improvements, and so on, later.

Refer to Market Research Databases

PROFESSIONAL ORGANIZATIONS

In addition to brokerage firms, industry organizations also offer market information. While brokers provide the

Do Your Tenants Shop Prada or Target?

The National Association of Realtors (www.
nar.realtor) provides demographic, industry, and housing reports for many urban and
suburban markets throughout the United
States (click on the website's "Research and
Statistics" tab). Although neighborhood
demographics exert less of an influence on
commercial real estate than on the residential sector, they are still important because of
their impact on workplace quality of life.[3]

best deal-specific information, other groups have valuable
demographic and industry statistics. Once again, organizations divide themselves between national entities with
more generic market information and local entities that
delve into the specifics of a market.

ACCESS SUBSCRIPTION DATABASES

In recent years, the real estate industry has been transformed by online market information, especially in the
form of subscription-based services. Companies with
online property databases publish and sell market data
that can be sliced and diced in a myriad of ways. Behemoth
firms dominate this knowledge industry, employing hundreds of researchers and infiltrating every major market. Other firms sell information they have amassed via
crowdsourcing.

In addition to listing comparables, some online subscription services offer detailed information regarding

building ownership, stacking plans, square footage, and more. With the touch of a finger, real estate professionals can take a virtual walk through a suite. These electronic tools can accelerate your learning and provide a strong foundation to precede firsthand visits to properties. Still, any subscription service is only as good as its contributors. While database companies have large research staffs and professional photographers, they remain somewhat reliant on industry insiders to confirm information. Very few leases are publicly recorded, meaning that most are fully accessible only to the landlord's real estate and legal departments, the tenant, and the broker, if involved. Many landlords hold information close to the vest, reluctant to lessen a potential competitive edge. Some report only portions of a deal without disclosing all of the details.

There is an inherent tension between database companies and brokers, as the subscription services assist brokers with malleable information but also act as a competitor of

---

Newsies

Buy a subscription to the local paper(s)—especially smaller publications—to frame the business and political landscape. You'll learn which companies are growing, the stance on business, and juicy real estate scoop. Although newspapers can lag the marketplace by up to six months—an eternity in real estate—and can fail to report full deal details, they do provide another data point for your market information.

sorts by publishing information previously held exclusively by industry insiders. Because so much of the value of brokers lies in their knowledge, they are reluctant to give up information that might compromise a competitive advantage, the most significant of which are deal comparables (the terms of signed lease deals). So while increasing numbers of real estate professionals subscribe to database services and the technology becomes more and more robust, many still consider the brokerage community's word on the street to be the definitive source of real estate information.

PLACE THE MARKET IN CONTEXT

After completing your local market research, step back to consider the market—and its timing—as a whole. This consideration allows you to place your property in context of the overall market. Because of real estate's illiquidity, professionals need to weather markets, strong and weak. For example, leasing veterans who have been scarred with the memory of a bad market protect their downside by making deals that can stand the test of cyclical supply and demand. They maintain good relationships, pay close attention to lease clauses, and watch their wallets. For the long term, leasing professionals examine the lease from two angles: First, how does the deal look in today's market? Second, will the deal remain solid if—and when—the market turns?

Cycles can be both protracted and extreme, as real estate and construction link arms in a dance of supply and demand. The real estate market, like the stock market, tends to be buoyed during periods of economic growth and depressed when the economy contracts. In bull markets, growing companies create excess demand for space; in bear markets, businesses, along with demand for space, can shrink significantly. Wharton professors Richard Herring and Susan Wachter write, "real estate cycles may occur simply because of forecast errors and lags in the adjustment of the stock of commercial structures," and they note the two to six years required for new construction.[4] Another study predicts market fluctuations on a ten-year cycle.[5] Regardless of the exact length of time, recognizing the cyclical nature of real estate markets can affect behavior as you recognize that deals—not to mention relationships and your capital reserves—have to stand the test of both tight and soft markets.

Moreover, extreme highs and lows characterize the industry. Not all markets are created equal; traditionally, the office market sector has been the most volatile, followed by the retail and the industrial sectors, respectively.[6] Further, submarkets experience varying levels of magnitude. Temperature aside, Phoenix may be hot while Denver wants for tenants. The takeaway: real estate requires a strong stomach and careful attention to deals that can stand the tests of time and market volatility.

Beyond the obvious fact that more concessions— mainly rent—will be given in a soft market and fewer concessions in a tight market, grizzled real estate veterans enjoy a tremendous advantage because of their long-term mindsets. It is one thing to intellectualize changing markets and quite another to endure the painful reality of a "see-through" building, empty of tenants. Over time, these cycles sear reality onto our collective leasing memories.

Hot marketplaces can obliterate long-term memory. As an example of shortsightedness, when my firm announced a large lease in a newspaper ad, our marketing director, giddy with her new title, opined that we did not "owe" the broker gratitude by listing his name. She felt that paying the broker his commission was sufficient. I lobbied hard to name the brokerage company because I knew that when the market turned, we would rely on strong brokerage relationships to bring us tenants. Why not reinforce connections when we have the luxury of doing so? Consider the example of Jack Welch, the former CEO of General Electric. He took pains to thank employees on plant tours and facility visits in order to strengthen the company culture.[7] Gratitude reinforces relationships that serve companies well, especially in tough economic times.

Set Boots on the Ground

With your new perspective, of both the local marketplace and the industry cycle, you are ready to study the market more on a firsthand basis.

IDENTIFY COMPETING PROPERTIES

Your local market competitors are the properties of like quality and location that will offer space to prospective tenants. In terms of location, there's not a set circumference for a competitive boundary; it's more often a neighborhood, such as a financial district or an area with sprawling office parks. Real estate brokers define a neighborhood with their own, sometimes seemingly arbitrary, criteria. While it may not make sense to a market outsider, factors such as freeways, traffic flow, square-footage concentration, businesses, amenities, and cultural differences all play roles in shaping real estate brokers' definition of a neighborhood. By speaking with local brokers, you'll come to understand how one neighborhood varies from another, with corresponding differences in rent and desirability.

For businesses, transportation in all its incarnations (freeway access, public transportation, surface streets, and parking) can delineate a neighborhood. It is therefore important to examine the freeways, bus routes, the metro/rail system, and topography to gain an understanding of a neighborhood's access.

Next, try to learn which types of industries dominate the marketplace. For instance, a city with a large refinery will differ greatly from a town hovering in the shadow of an insurance giant. The type of businesses and employees an area attracts will drive its local commercial real estate markets.

Further, survey the community for its amenities. Public and private businesses enjoy proximity to amenities that enrich the lives of their employees. Is there a local athletic club? What types of restaurants and stores line the streets? By understanding the local amenities, you will gain an appreciation of the types of businesses that enjoy a neighborly relationship.

When the San Francisco Law Library moved its offices from one downtown building to another, law firms followed suit. Later, as technology allowed for the electronic storage of reference materials, the need for a physical library diminished. When it did, so did the demand for proximate office space. The moral of the story? Amenities can create demand for office space.[8]

Next, examine the quality of construction and the types of amenities of nearby properties to determine which buildings will act as competition in your neighborhood.

By listening to brokers speak about buildings, reading marketing materials, and driving (or walking) around the neighborhood, you can fairly easily determine if a building is similar enough to your own to qualify as a competitor.

DO YOU KNOW THESE DETAILS ABOUT YOUR COMPETITION?

☐ Building name, address, and owner
☐ Current space availability, including the size and quality of the spaces
☐ Advertised rent
☐ Leasing company
☐ Parking
☐ Square footage
☐ Major tenants
☐ Amenities, including special features of the building
☐ Management company
☐ Lease comparables

VISIT LOCAL BUILDINGS

For a real education on your local marketplace, nothing compares to firsthand visits to competing buildings. For instance, while glossy brochures may highlight a beautiful garden rooftop, a tour might unearth the building's lack of parking—something marketers won't advertise. You can drive or walk a neighborhood (especially a suburban one) on a Sunday and skip the traffic jams. You may not be able to gain lobby access, but it's an expedient way to get a sense of the market prior to a more thorough study. Do, though, make sure to revisit the property during the week, to get a sense of its operations during business hours. By standing

> ### Start at the Top
>
> Consider starting at the top of the building and working your way down. That way, if security ushers you from the building, you have seen more of the property than had you started at the lower floors. Security concerns can restrict free access to office buildings in urban and governmental areas, so if you can't access the entire building, at a minimum, visit the lobby and read the tenant directory.

in the tenant's shoes, you gain an understanding of a property's attributes, good and bad.

When you visit a property, treat it as if you work in the building every day. By driving and parking (or taking transit), examining the tenant directory, ordering something from the café, seeing how well bathrooms are maintained, and taking an elevator, you'll get a sense of the quality of the building and its maintenance. Snap a photo of the building and take some notes. Because tours and the ensuing lease decisions are often predicated on a brief visit, your investigation will likely mirror a typical prospect's experience. Your first impressions will inform you as to how your own property compares to competitor's buildings.

CHAPTER 2

Position the Property

"It takes a lot of unspectacular
preparation to have spectacular results."[1]
—*Roger Staubach, executive chairman, Jones Lang LaSalle*

GOAL: POSITION THE PROPERTY TO
COMPETE SUCCESSFULLY AGAINST
OTHER BUILDINGS THAT LEASE SPACE IN
THE LOCAL MARKET

Once you have gathered information about your neighborhood, the competing buildings, and the local real estate
market, you need to examine your own building(s) and
rent terms to assess and position them for leasing success.

Evaluate Your Property

CONSIDER ATTRIBUTES AND AMENITIES

By considering the attributes and amenities of your property, you become uniquely positioned to advertise its strengths. Start by identifying the traditional assets such as location, nearby amenities, great views, and architecturally pleasing features. Beyond that, try to relate your building attributes to your particular market. For instance, in congested urban areas, freeway and public-transportation access may be critical. Because parking can be extremely limited in such areas, easy public-transportation access and walkability may prove more valuable than an overpriced, crowded parking structure. Conversely, in suburban areas, tenants might see more value in freeway proximity and the ability to take alternate routes during commute hours. A parking structure or lot in this instance would be invaluable. Understanding the particular demands of your prospective tenants and highlighting the attributes of your property that meet them will help you market vacant space.

When you consider amenities, think large. They are often more than simply a great sushi restaurant or nearby fitness club. For example, when Visa Inc. searched for its national headquarters, the company settled on the San Francisco Peninsula.[2] Why did Visa choose one of the most expensive areas of the country? Because of its proximity to the highly educated workforce available from nearby Stanford University and the University of California, Berkeley. From Visa's perspective, local intellectual capital was a valuable asset that gave Foster City a sharp competitive edge.[3] Visa also considered that Foster City ranked as one of *Forbes* magazine's "Top Towns to Live Well," which

Flaunt It If You've Got It

Determine the top three attributes of your property and highlight these in your marketing materials and pitch. Public-transportation access? Excellent property management? The granddaddy of them all: location?

might encourage employees to put down roots.[4] As you evaluate a property, always assess its surrounding features: an educated workforce, housing, entertainment, access, livability, and so on.

EVALUATE (AND ADD) SUSTAINABILITY

How green is your building? Sustainability has become a key feature in most office markets. Heightened concern for the environment, moreover, reflects the desires of many company leaders who hail from the so-called millennial generation, a generation said to desire concrete solutions to environmental challenges while working in a place "aligned with their values."[5] Contemporary company leaders tend to care deeply about environmental issues, and these values strongly influence their real estate decisions.

Green practices improve space desirability, employee retention, and operating expenses, all of which affect a prospective tenant's leasing decisions. Economically, green benefits that reduce operating expenses can give landlords a leasing edge over non-environmentally minded properties because savings may be passed back to tenants. For example, an open floor plenum can reduce heating and cooling expenses and yield operating-cost savings that can be passed on to the tenant. A leasing professional who can understand and communicate this aspect of value gained as a result of green building will enjoy a tremendous leasing edge, particularly in down markets.

Industry research indicates that tenants feel happier in green environments. A study from the University of San Diego's business school surveyed 154 buildings with approximately two thousand tenants and found that employees in green buildings enjoyed 2.88 fewer sick days per year and a 4.88 percent productivity increase. There's also the real, if difficult to quantify, green effect that improves employee morale—simply, a sense that a green building is a nicer place to work and can translate into improved employee retention rates.[6]

Increasingly, landlords are focusing on sustainability features to ensure they have a competitive place in the market. While individual landlords' green practices may vary widely—from expensive heating, venting, and air conditioning (HVAC) implementations to basic paper-recycling programs—buildings without any green attributes now seem dated and compete at a disadvantage. Energy Star certified buildings—those that use less energy and emit less carbon dioxide than typical buildings—are now widely found in Los Angeles, Washington, DC, Dallas, Atlanta, and New York, and are becoming more common-place throughout the United States.[7] Commercial building owners can enjoy substantial tax credits in exchange for achieving measurable green building goals.[8] In today's leasing climate, a building's sustainable attributes are important features when presenting a property to the market.

On the other side of the coin, any environmental hazards must be understood and disclosed in the marketing process. Items such as asbestos or groundwater

Green, by LEED

Established in 1992, the US Green Building Council (USGBC) offers the LEED (Leadership in Energy and Environmental Design) certification, the industry yardstick of green construction and practices. When a building wears a LEED plaque on its exterior, it indicates that the property meets a complicated set of sustainability criteria. Certifications range from the highest-level platinum to gold to silver. In addition, contractors can earn LEED certification for their environmental practices. Because LEED certification is costly and time consuming, some landlords prefer to adopt and advertise green practices while forgoing a formal designation.

contamination are of major interest to most corporate tenants and can stop a deal in its tracks. Because of the legalities and exposure (no pun intended) associated with these issues, it's best to consult your legal counsel.

Establish Competitive Lease Terms

A building's value is calculated based on its assured rental income stream. For an existing building, leasing professionals study the rent roll—the summary of all the leases in the building—that lists tenants and their square footage, location, rent, lease expiration date, and encumbrances (such as a right to expand or a right to renew) that may burden other spaces in the property, in order to gain perspective on a property's leasing status. The rent roll reveals how much of the building is leased, to whom, and at what rates, while also exposing vacancies and space vulnerabilities such as several leases expiring at the same time. Also, a holistic look at the building gives you information about market rental rates and typical tenant sizes for your property.

For both occupied and vacant buildings, creating the right mix of tenants, carving vacant spaces into leasable chunks, setting term lengths, and establishing rent and other improvement allowances all require a delicate balance. While each landlord's particular ownership goals will guide decisions with regard to the final terms of a given lease, there are common components of the central business terms of most leases.

TENANT MIX

A complementary tenant mix can both attract businesses to particular buildings and, once there, help them flourish. For instance, a medical building's marketing plan might target physicians, dentists, laboratories, radiologists, and a pharmacy. A more generic office building within blocks of the train station and close to restaurants and bars might appeal to technology firms with employees that use public transit. And an iconic property such as San Francisco's Transamerica Pyramid may attract a veritable Who's Who of investment firms, law firms, banks, and venture capitalists. Good landlords cultivate a tenant mix that supports the financial well-being of their tenants. After all, healthy tenants make for rent-collecting landlords. It is thus essential to define the optimal tenant mix for the property, paying attention to the companies that populate the market.

The flip side of the tenant mix equation is occupants who detract from others' experiences at the property. Be wary of leasing to tenants who use a disproportionate amount of resources at the expense of others. For instance, the tenant who monopolizes the freight elevator with frequent deliveries will irritate the tenants who want easy elevator access for their clients. While specific businesses such as a restaurant may insist on a non-compete clause within the property, most tenants leave this issue of appropriate tenant mix to the landlord's judgment. Again, as a practical matter, intelligent landlords consider the well-being of their existing tenants before leasing to companies that might cannibalize those tenants' businesses and jeopardize their ability to pay rent. In addition, leasing a majority of building space to tenants in a particular industry sector may make a building more susceptible. For example, buildings largely leased to finance companies, mortgage brokers, and so on experienced greater vacancy and bankruptcy proceedings during the economic downturn of the past decade than did buildings with highly diversified tenant rosters.

SUITE SIZE

Deciding how (or if) to carve vacant space into leasable suites requires balancing factors such as market demand, the building's design, and the owner's willingness to accept the vulnerability of one or more concurrent lease expirations. Offering spaces in particular sizes can be a Rubik's Cube of planning, with the realities of daily leasing and market demand upending even the best-laid plans.

There is a relationship between suite size and term length. In order to assemble large blocks of leasable space, you need expiration dates to coincide or you need to negotiate a relocation clause for existing tenants so you can accommodate large or expanding companies. For example, suppose you have Tenant A with 15,000 square feet adjacent to Tenant B with 3,000 square feet. In order to assure maximum flexibility for the larger tenant that might need more space, a landlord might want to keep the smaller tenant's lease term coincidental with the larger tenant's or, at minimum, obtain a relocation clause. A relocation clause, if exercised, can be expensive (and create unhappiness on the part of the relocated tenant), so many landlords consider it a last resort even though they often have this (relocation) clause in their standard lease forms. So it's not that landlords will not exercise this right, generally they just prefer to avoid it. Some owners prefer to carve up one floor for smaller tenants and retain larger blocks of space for the big fish in the marketplace. These are calculated risks, but leasing professionals must make these types of decisions every day.

Awareness of Existing Tenant Rights

When strategizing about how to offer space to the market, it's important to understand any existing tenant rights. Oftentimes, vacant space is *encumbered*, meaning there's an existing obligation to another party with respect to the space. For instance, a current tenant may have a right of first offer, right of refusal, or an expansion right on an adjacent suite. As you market the vacant suite, you need to offer the vacant space within the parameters already set forth in the current tenant's lease. Savvy landlords need to understand under what terms they can place vacant space on the market.

I once negotiated a lease for an 80,000 square-foot space, which entailed moving five tenants—yes, five—none of whom had a formal relocation clause in their lease. How did I do it? I moved them to more desirable spaces or cut a better rent deal with them, and of course I paid moving expenses. After a bottle of aspirin and many late nights of negotiation, I was able to assemble the large block of space for a lucrative ten-year lease. That experience taught me the value of relocation clauses, especially in buildings with floor plates suited to large tenants.

TERM LENGTH

In the commercial sector, five-year lease terms are typical, with a preference (and occasionally rent discounts) for seven- or ten-year terms. In general, landlords prefer lengthy lease terms because of the assured stream of rental income.

Also, typically, the higher the level of tenant improvements, the longer the lease term an owner will want, in order to allow for the amortization of capital investment, especially for customized space. On the other hand, a landlord might offer space with a shorter lease duration, especially when tenants take the space *as is* or with minimal investment, when a space has proved difficult to lease, or when a short-term tenant acts as a placeholder of sorts, paying rent on space that might ultimately be absorbed by other existing tenants.

Alternatively, a landlord may choose to lease an entire property to a single tenant—wonderful for rental return but perhaps vulnerable for lease renewal as the lease expiration nears and the landlord faces the prospect of a completely or mostly vacant building. On the other hand, varying lease expiration terms create more balance but can also limit the landlord's ability to assemble a large block of space in a single offering. In the end, though, decisions on term length are based less on landlord preference and more on the demand in the marketplace.

In San Francisco's hip South of Market area, innovative leasing is alive and well. There, RocketSpace offers thousands of square feet of incubator space to over 130 seed-funded technology start-ups. The space provides flexible offices, technology support, and a community of tech innovators. The vibe is young and irreverent, as illustrated by the chalkboard directions that point Future World Leaders in one direction and Insecure Geniuses in another.

Blend and Extend

Oftentimes, existing tenants seek lower rents when the market has dropped considerably since the initial lease signature, or because of different circumstances in their own business. Landlords in such situations may want to "blend and extend" a new lower (mix of the old and new rates) rent in exchange for a longer lease term. While the landlord's immediate rental income stream may decrease, the security of a longer lease term offsets the reduced rent. For example, assume an existing tenant has a five-year lease term. Several years into the lease, the market drops out and competing buildings entice your tenant with offers of lower rental rates. The tenant cringes at the existing high rental rate and resentment builds. While it might be perfectly reasonable for the landlord to argue that the lease's rate was fair at the time of signing, a better strategy often is to reduce the tenant's rental rate to that of (or closer to) the current market rate, and to blend the old and new rates over an extended lease term.

The tenant wins because the rent is now consistent with the market. The landlord wins because the tenant's term has been extended (possibly without incurring a brokerage commission and tenant improvements), thus creating value, and the rent is still at a competitive market rate. The landlord's initial tenant improvements and other capital investments will still be amortized, albeit over a longer term, and the possibility of incurring new capital expenses in connection with replacement tenants will have been minimized.

RENT

Probably more than any other aspect of the lease, tenants, landlords, and brokers focus on rent. Setting the appropriate rate positions your property for success. Although it's a bit academic (because net rent is actually a calculation determined by a variety of factors), the face rental rate is typically what is advertised and, oftentimes, first reported for a lease. So while you learn the complexities behind the face rental rate and learn that a lease's value depends on a variety of economic factors, you need to acknowledge the high profile the market gives to this number.

Leasing plans establish a pro forma rent, the rental income needed to service the building's debt, pay its utilities, and operate the property with positive cash flow. Usually, pro formas are determined during the development or purchase period of a building and can evolve with changes in the loan structure and operating costs. But regardless of any pro forma, rental rates will necessarily reflect only what the competitive market will bear. It is therefore critical to understand comparables in the marketplace in order to set a rental rate that can compete with other buildings.

The property lender can exert a significant influence on a building's leasing efforts too. Nowadays, there's a growing trend of lenders having approval rights over lease deals exceeding a certain size or term or varying more than an allowed percentage below pro forma. Of course, these requirements vary from lender to lender (and property to property).

With an understanding of the various iterations of rent such as net rental rate, blended new and old rates (in a lease renewal), and the impact of capital improvements on rental rates, you can craft a stronger overall lease.

Face Rent Versus Net Effective Rent

Real estate leasing professionals differentiate between the (face) rental rate and the (net) effective rental rate. The *face rent* is the nominal rental amount listed on the lease. The *net effective rent* is the actual rent once any tenant inducements such as free rent (also called abated rent), reduced rent, and higher tenant improvement allowances are taken into account. Any landlord concession that reduces the tenant's rent obligation affects the net effective rent.

Because many office leases are *gross leases*, meaning they include operating expenses and, often, tenant inducements, it can take some arithmetic to uncover the net effective rental rate. For example, suppose you rent a suite for $36 per square foot per year for a three-year lease term, and you give your new tenant six months of free rent at the commencement of the term. While the face rent is $36 per square foot, the net effective rent is $30 per square foot per year, as you only collect rent for thirty months (rather than thirty-six) once the free rent is factored in.

Keep in mind that the time value of money also needs to be considered, as for instance, six months of free rent today (assuming a constant rental rate) is costlier to the landlord than six months of free rent spread over the entire term of the lease. That's because giving free rent initially denies the landlord use of those funds for investment, while spreading the rent concession over the term allows the landlord to use (invest) that money in the intervening time.

Landlords tend to pay attention to face rents because these are often the rent comparables quoted in the marketplace. Also, when tenants renew leases, they often refer to the face value of the rent for renewal comparisons, neglecting (or forgetting) to calculate the true effective rent. Generally speaking, the higher a face rent, the better the deal appears for the landlord.

Whether leases are gross leases, triple net leases (exclusive of operating expenses which the tenant pays), or economic triple net (in which the landlord still provides the services), the point is that you'll need to unravel the various lease concessions to ascertain the true net effective rent of any lease.

Saving Face

While leasing agents may quote the face rental rate as they exchange comparables, know that the effective rental rate is the true rate that matters in terms of value and return on investment.

So setting rental rates becomes a nuanced process because *all* the economic factors of a deal, including tenant improvements, architectural fees, brokerage commissions, any periods of free rent, the lease term, and so on, conspire to affect the effective (net) rental rate. And, a good leasing agent can make a better net deal by streamlining tenant improvements or renewing a tenant sans brokerage commission, thus raising the net effective rental rate. To further complicate a building's return, one tenant's slightly lower rental rate can be offset by a more profitable rental rate of another tenant, making the building finances as a whole workable for the landlord. So while face rental rates have their purpose, wise leasing agents focus on net effective rates.

I once turned market knowledge into gold during lease renewals. I had a suburban property outside the limits—and tax jurisdiction—of a city that imposed payroll taxes on businesses, thus creating lower effective rental rates for my property. So I created a chart comparing our effective rent to the city-rent-plus-taxes number. The exercise so effectively exposed hidden costs, that my tenants— especially those with large payrolls—often chose to stay instead of moving inside the city limits.

Rent Prices Can Connote Value

Because each lease deal is different in terms of the capital required, many landlords advertise rent as a range, with the ultimate rate a function of tenant improvements and other financial components.

Pricing involves a mix of market knowledge and psychology, much of it backed by studies. For instance, a Yale

University study found that tiered pricing choices led to buyers making more decisions to purchase.[9] That tiered pricing may represent suites throughout a building, from the penthouse to a subterranean space for call centers. While long-term leasing decisions certainly differ from selling packs of gum, for example, research also implies that psychology impacts purchase choices, leading sellers to price goods and services accordingly. As a practical example, buyers often make a correlation between price and quality. Thus, raising rent or keeping rent near the upper end of your competitive marketplace may connote value in the eyes of a prospective client.

In a classic example of tenants equating quality with cost, I worked on a 15,000 square foot lease for a technology firm that didn't feel quite comfortable with our building architect. In an effort to win over the tenant, the architect offered to draw the conceptual space plans for free (with the belief the tenant would like the design and proceed with the complete plans). The plan, however, backfired. The tenant told me that if an architect was willing to work for free, he probably wasn't much good. This taught me that undercharging or not charging for work can undermine the perception of one's value. That's why I decided to keep our rental rates on the upper side of the competitive market scale.

OPERATING EXPENSES

Landlords determine which operating expenses are included in the base rent and which are paid directly by the tenant. "Gross" or "full service" leases mean that the landlord provides and pays for the utilities and other expenses incumbent in running a building. Typically, landlords seek reimbursement for a pro rata share (according to the tenant's square footage) of expenses or of increase in expenses. Other leases though, exclude operating expenses, in a "net" or "triple net" arrangement. Buildings usually follow market trend with regard to the structure of operating expenses relative to the lease.

TENANT IMPROVEMENTS

Tenant improvements, which constitute the lion's share of capital leasing costs for most commercial properties, are, in essence, the price landlords must pay to take raw or outdated space to market-ready space. Depending on the location (urban or suburban), unionized or non-unionized labor, material costs, and so on, the cost of tenant improvements can range widely. Once installed, tenant improvements are permanently affixed to the building and, as such, are considered part of the property. They usually add value assuming the improvements are generic enough that they could be used by a variety of tenants in the marketplace.

Turnkey Versus Tenant Improvement Allowance

Leasing professionals should understand the differences between turnkey and allowance-based tenant improvements and, ultimately, decide on the structure that makes the best sense in their marketplaces. In a turnkey arrangement, the landlord constructs the space according to an approved space plan using standardized finishes (often displayed on a physical finish board with carpet, paint, and other samples). For the vast majority of tenants in this scenario, the construction price is somewhat irrelevant as they focus on the office's form and function. With turnkey construction, the tenant doesn't have to worry if improvement dollars are adequate to construct the desired space, because the landlord guarantees such. Few tenants care about or have construction experience, and they prefer to focus on their primary business. Turnkey construction requires a landlord who understands building design and costs and has a reliable contractor who can construct a space on time and within budget. In addition, turnkey deals require good control over the tenant who may try to make costly (or time consuming) changes to the approved plan.

In contrast, in a deal with a tenant improvement allowance, the landlord agrees to contribute a specific dollar amount for construction. The tenant may also contribute funds for construction of the tenant improvements in the suite. Then, although the landlord generally manages the construction, the tenant is responsible for any tenant improvement expenses over the cost of the allowance. Should the tenant improvement project finish under budget, the tenant may receive a credit. This scenario usually implies an involved tenant—with a line-by-line understanding of the construction estimate—who is responsible for any expenses over the allotted tenant improvement allowance.

Americans with Disabilities Act Compliance

Sometimes, in order to construct a tenant space, common area expenses—notably Americans with Disabilities Act (ADA) compliance—are incurred. Depending upon the nature of the changes, the expenses may be charged to the new tenant or, perhaps, assessed to the building as a whole.

Expense Comparisons

For benchmarks of capital and operating expenses across 5,400 buildings in 250 distinct markets, refer to the Experience Exchange. *Report* published and sold by the Building Owners and Managers Association (BOMA).

BROKERAGE COMMISSIONS

After tenant improvements, the next largest capital expenditure is usually the commission paid to the brokerage representing the tenant. Brokerage commissions are set by negotiation, according to your competitive marketplace, and typically follow one of two structures: a percentage of rent or a set dollar amount per term (e.g., $5 per square foot for a five-year term). Commissions are usually remitted one half when the lease is signed and one half when the tenant takes occupancy. Commissions are generally owed to both the listing broker and the procuring—or outside—broker. (See chapter 4, Work with Brokers, for more discussion on commissions.)

SOFT COSTS: ARCHITECTURAL FEES AND MARKETING EXPENSES

Known as soft costs, architectural fees, such as space planning, and marketing costs are other expenses associated with leasing space. As a general rule, space planning runs less than $1 per square foot, depending on the marketplace. Should the tenant sign a lease, full architectural construction documents add several more dollars per square foot to the leasing costs.

Marketing expenses run the gamut and they, too, are considered soft costs, meaning that they are necessary to sell the space but can be difficult to quantify and thus attribute to any particular deal. For example, how should you assess the impact of a quality property flier? While marketing expenses may be distributed on a pro rata share basis per square foot, the reality is that marketing pieces may not benefit all vacant spaces equally. Such pieces, however, are considered the price you pay to compete in the marketplace. Now it's up to you to decide which pieces are worthwhile to market your property.

CHAPTER 3

Develop Marketing Materials

"There is more similarity in a precious painting by Degas and
a frosted mug of root beer than you ever thought possible."[1]
—*A. Alfred Taubman, retail real estate developer*

GOAL: TO CREATE EFFECTIVE AND
APPROPRIATE MARKETING MATERIALS
FOR PROPERTIES

Professional leasing personnel know they need materials
that show a property to its best advantage. While a marketing package can range from fuzzy snapshots to photographs that are the envy of *Architectural Digest,* most
owners assemble advertising pieces depending on the
amount of available space, the market conditions, and their
budget. Basics include online space availability listings and
a bare-bones property flier, while a full marketing package contains an array of pieces that promote a building

or, oftentimes, a portfolio of properties. The variety can satisfy requirements ranging from short-term leasing (by announcing space availability and amenities) to long-term industry branding. While not mutually exclusive, these short- and long-term goals do require thoughtful design, efficient production, and a consistent message. Although online resources have revolutionized production, basic good design and quality materials should underpin all your marketing efforts.

Assemble a Suite of Marketing Materials

The following list contains a menu of potential marketing options to consider, depending on the space available for lease and the marketing budget (in loosely descending order of importance and/or complexity):

- ☐ Space availability listing (electronic and possibly printed)
- ☐ One-page property flier (usually with photograph)
- ☐ Leasing signs
- ☐ Floor plans and stacking plans of suites (including electronic versions)
- ☐ Amenity sheet (including transit opportunities)
- ☐ Aerial photograph
- ☐ Maps
- ☐ Folder to hold it all (may have property logo or embossed label)
- ☐ Website
- ☐ Property logo
- ☐ Stationery (with property address)
- ☐ Newspaper advertising
- ☐ Postcard
- ☐ Credibility wall
- ☐ Finish board with building-standard paint colors, carpet, stone, etc.

SPACE AVAILABILITY LISTING

Space availabilities list current or upcoming vacancies and include the square footage and a brief description of the space. Landlords typically publish these space availabilities online via listing services as well as on their own websites. Additionally, landlords sometimes publish a printed sheet of such availabilities for brokers or prospective tenants.

Online and printed listings, however, have limitations because of the information grapevine so prevalent in real estate. To illustrate, consider shadow space—the sublease space not formally on the market. These types of sublease spaces may be in quiet flux, with swirling rumors. For instance, companies planning to downsize may not tell their employees in advance, fearing an exodus. But brokers and owners who know of the possible available space may have prospects lined up for the pending vacancy. Boom!

The Important Profile Pic

Many prospective tenants, even when represented by brokers, conduct their own online searches to get a feel for the market. Make sure your property looks appealing with current information, high-resolution photographs, your property logo, etc. Some of the online listing services allow customization and design services, so ask.

The deal is done before reaching the public. The inefficiencies of online listing services become pronounced in tight markets where firsthand knowledge and relationships best an electronic service. In a soft market, however, online leasing services become more relevant as landlords engage every available tool to fill vacancies.

Double-Click for (Almost) Instant Fliers

Online listing services often offer cost-effective packages such as a design template and printing for a property flier. Upload a photograph of the building, insert information into the spaces available and—voilà—you have a professional quality flier that can be posted online or printed.

ONE-PAGE PROPERTY FLIER

The workhorse of advertisements, a single-page flier typically includes a color photograph, bulleted points highlighting the property's attributes, leasing contact information, and occasionally, a map or floor plan (often on the back of the flier). These fliers can be printed or electronic, or both.

LEASING SIGNS

Generally four-by-eight-foot (standard size) pieces of painted plywood, these signs are placed near the parking entrance or in the exterior landscaping near the building for lease. For urban locations, leasing agents display large poster reproductions in windows. Designed to capture a motorist's attention, the lettering must be extremely legible, so be sure to check fonts, sizes, and colors for readability.

IS YOUR LEASING SIGN EFFECTIVE?

☐ Minimize text by including the basics only: *Leasing* or *Space Available*, a contact name, and a telephone number.

☐ Make letters at least six inches tall for legibility.

☐ Choose dark (or strongly colored) text on a light background for readability.

☐ Use applied vinyl letters with reflective material for nighttime visibility.

FLOOR PLANS AND STACKING PLANS

The floor plan shows the tenant the boundaries of a specific suite (sometimes within the larger context of the entire floor) and illustrates the entry, private offices, conference rooms, kitchen, and so on. Floor plans typically note the suite number, building address, and *rentable* square footage of a particular suite. Stacking plans are numerous floor plans combined, which indicate the layout of the floors and contain a visual representation of the building's configuration and tenants.

In today's market, professionals often display floor plans on backlit screens of a mobile device. With the swipe of a finger, the broker can present color images of similar suites completely finished and furnished to deepen a tenant's understanding of how an office might look for a particular company.

> ## Noting the Rentable Square Footage
>
> Many landlords list only the *rentable* square footage (the *usable* square footage plus a pro rata share of the common areas) on floor plans because rent is based on that measurement. Noting the usable square footage prompts prospects to focus on the *load factor*, the differential between usable and rentable square footage, derived from common areas. There's not much you can do about a building's load factor, so emphasizing it doesn't usually work to the landlord's advantage.

AMENITY SHEET

Amenity sheets list nearby resources such as restaurants, shops, banks, childcare, post offices, hospitals, transportation, health clubs, and so on. Oftentimes, the various categories listed above are color coded. Amenity sheets should be revised and updated twice a year (and as needed) to reflect the current neighborhood.

AERIAL PHOTOGRAPH

An aerial photograph of the property, enlarged and mounted on one-half-inch-thick poster board (or projected onto a large screen in your conference room while you provide details), is one of the most effective marketing tools in the industry. Lightweight and portable, it also travels well to accompany a tour group meeting in the lobby or to an easel in the marketing office.

MAPS

Leasing personnel use maps to identify a particular building's location and to call attention to the surrounding amenities and transportation access. By highlighting restaurants, banks, post offices, shopping centers, trains, bus stops, and freeway access in various colors, landlords underscore a wealth of services for prospective tenants in any given location. Use an editor's eye to make the map informative and legible.

FOLDER

Create a polished, professional look by inserting printed marketing materials into a quality folder. Emboss folders with your company name or the property name. As an alternative, some landlords create a large label with the property's address and logo, print it in color, and adhere it to a generic folder, which is now customized.

Presenting Marketing Materials

When presenting marketing materials, hand your business card to the prospect separately. Business protocol will encourage prospects to give you their card in exchange, in the event they have not handed you one already.

WEBSITE

Landlords routinely establish websites for individual properties as a way of promoting the property and its virtues. If your company does not have a webmaster, freelance vendors offer inexpensive and effective services to advertise space and collect prospects. Even the most basic websites boast a building photograph, property description, amenity list, and contact information.

Additionally, websites can display a virtual tour to show visitors the available space. Although a seasickness sensation continues to plague virtual reality technology, many architectural firms and landlords (especially those catering to international businesses) now use this option to introduce a space to prospects.

> *I love the creative virtual tour of one San Francisco high-rise. From the comfort of an armchair, prospective tenants enter the lobby, ride the elevator, and walk to the window to see the panoramic penthouse view.*
>
> *More recently, I watched a one-minute time-lapse video of the San Francisco Museum of Modern Art's renovation—from dirt excavation to sculpture installation—if only real-life construction moved that quickly![2] It was an inspiring piece, set to music, and I can imagine other property development sites using a similar approach to captivate tenants and prospects.*

PROPERTY LOGO

Marketing plans can include a logo, designed to create a distinctive identity for a property or real estate portfolio.

When a property has its own logo, it is usually placed on multiple pieces, such as the letterhead, property flier, leasing sign, and other marketing collateral. Additionally, the logo may be printed on the walk-off mat at the entry, the building directory, and so on.

STATIONERY

Using quality paper stock and letterhead creates a consistent look, particularly when various marketing pieces are assembled into a package. Remember that the envelopes should match the paper. In general, ivory or white (considered more modern) paper creates a professional appearance and contrasts against dark text for maximum legibility.

NEWSPAPER ADVERTISING

When advertising in a newspaper, consider size, placement (business section, upper part of page, etc.), frequency, and rate. Inexpensive spot color works especially well on newspaper print. Try surrounding your ad with a color border or use spot color to call attention to your logo and company

---

Spot Color: An Inexpensive Alternative

Many newspapers and other advertising media offer spot color (one color in addition to black and white) at a minimal cost. Cheaper than full color, it's usually more effective than black and white alone.

name. Also, discuss placement with the newspaper representative to ensure that your single- or one-color image does not play runner-up by being placed near a four-color "beauty queen" advertisement.

TOMBSTONE AD

Tombstone advertisements are smallish ads surrounded by a border, oftentimes commemorating a lease deal or sale. They are generally used by landlords to announce the tenant and acknowledge the transaction team (usually the procuring and listing brokers) for significantly sized leases.

POSTCARD

A long-standing and cost-effective (because postcards qualify for inexpensive bulk mailing) marketing tool, most postcards contain a photograph with contact information. By displaying a high-quality photo and using standard fonts, landlords can avoid the hallmarks of cheap postcards—numerous fonts, too-small photographs, and excessive punctuation.

CREDIBILITY WALL

Credibility walls include framed displays of property photographs with building names and locations identified on accompanying captions or plaques. The real estate company's name (or the building's name) might top the frame, often etched in stainless steel, chrome, bronze, wood, or Lucite. The wall typically hangs in a reception area and demonstrates a quality property portfolio and management to prospective tenants.

FINISH BOARD

Finish boards display building-standard paint colors, carpet, baseboard, stone, and so on. The board both shows
a building's commitment to quality finishes and makes
it easier for tenants to decide on finishes using a visual,
curated array.

Visual Design Fundamentals

Good design basics make it easy for the human eye to
digest information, best accomplished with an appealing
layout, effective copy, and memorable color. For the most
part, marketing pieces seek to lead brokers and prospective
clients to a landlord's leasing representative, so the pieces
tend to be direct and have high visual appeal.

LAYOUT

In terms of layout, the local ophthalmologist knows a
graphic design secret or two. In Western culture, our
eyes move from left to right and from top to bottom. As
a result, the most effective printed materials form a Z pattern. That's why so many ads display the most important
written information across the top of the page, have a photograph (or other image) on the upper right side, and con-
tinue with bullet points or other succinct language down
the left column and perhaps a tagline running horizontally
along the bottom of the piece.

In addition, a pleasing pattern of text and images contains white—or negative—space in which the eye has an
opportunity to rest. Effective designers use ample margin
widths and space between text and photos. For example,

> **The Z Layout**
> Some of the most effective printed materials display information and graphics in a Z-shaped pattern.

enlarging an image and limiting bullet points can prove more impactful than a bevy of information. While amateurs fill every available space, summon your inner Steve Jobs to appreciate the beauty of clean, curated pieces.

COLOR

Color theory—the study of the visual effect of specific color combinations—allows you to use design choices to evoke a desired response. For example, the color red can speed the pulse, increase the respiration rate, and raise blood pressure. Red is associated with words like *winner, achiever, intense, impulsive* and *active* but also *danger.* Think red neon in Las Vegas, prodding gamblers. Conservative blue suggests confidence, harmony, responsibility, and reliability. Think clear skies, calming travelers. In addition, each culture has its own color associations that influence perceptions and decisions. For instance, red might indicate prosperity and happiness in China yet signify mourning in South Africa. So cultural sensitivity matters.

Most marketing packages contain a variety of designs that can be produced in either color or black and white, depending on the purpose and cost. While color makes an advertisement more effective, its expense requires a cost-benefit analysis. Although your office's color-printer quality differs from a professional press run, many real

Color Your World

Pantone's website (www.pantone.com) shows what color can convey, with its descriptions of hues and their effects. As an industry influencer, Pantone designates an annual Color of the Year. Front-row New York Fashion Week tickets not included.

estate printing needs—such as fliers—can be accomplished with desktop technology.

When opting for professional printing, a full-color (also known as four-color) process uses magenta, cyan, yellow, and black in various combinations to produce images by running the paper through the printer numerous times. To select colors, graphic artists use the Pantone Matching System (PMS), which assigns a numerical value to each hue.[3] Its precise color identification ensures consistency throughout the printing phases so a regal red does not print as bubblegum pink.

FONTS

Typography refers to the way in which words are printed, including font style and legibility. An appropriate font connotes a style indicative of your property and management. For example, traditional fonts such as Garamond, Gill Sans, and Century indicate professionalism, while more askew fonts suggest whimsy. While the Jokerman font may prance around the pages of a preschool newsletter, building tenants may put more trust in a landlord who communicates in a traditional style using upright letters.

Talking Typeset

LEADING: the space between lines

SERIF: the traditional little lines at the tops and bottoms of letters

SANS SERIF: that's right, the little lines go missing

TYPOGRAPHY: the way printed words look, including font and readability choices

COPY: the text (as opposed to images)

Landlords sell a product that requires a high degree of efficiency: working elevators, clean windows, janitorial services, and so on. So pick a design commensurate with the property and its operation.

In addition to style, a font's readability is important. According to *Fortune* magazine, the average CEO of the Fortune 500 is fifty-eight years old.[4] Most middle-aged managers pack reading glasses, so make copy readable with 14-point (or larger) font and large, bold headlines. Black print proves the most legible on paper and especially

COOL IT ON THE CAPS

As anyone who has received an annoying text knows, using all capitals is the equivalent of shouting at your reader. Instead of caps, keep fonts to size 14 or larger to improve readability.

on light-colored computer screens. Also, limit font use to one or two styles. Or, consider a block font with upper- and lowercase letters for maximum readability. And refrain from excessive punctuation that resembles a teenager's text message more than a professional marketing piece.

PHOTOGRAPHY

In the flittering world of online bombardment, capturing attention proves more challenging than ever, so a photograph truly does speak a thousand words. Use images whenever possible when advertising vacant space. Whether you enlist a photographer or obtain a photograph from an existing bank, there are some practices that can improve the use of images.

> **In the flittering world of online bombardment, capturing attention proves more challenging than ever, so a photograph truly does speak a thousand words.**

Budget allowing, rely on professionals to photograph a property. Prices vary based on geography, but a building "glamour" shot should run less than a thousand dollars (and sometimes a few hundred) per photography session. Before committing to a contract, discuss the digital resolution and confirm that photo quality with your printer or technology department to ensure clear reproduction. Be aware that photographers can retain copyright ownership of the photograph, limiting your ability to use the image. Check that the contract allows unlimited use of the photograph, enabling reproduction on fliers, advertisements, postcard mailers, and online publications. Online photographic databases also offer images for purchase. Again, verify the copyright rules to avoid legal tussles over ownership and usage.

Next, primp the property for photo day. Make sure the building entrance is free of cars and delivery trucks. Some landlords specify showing a minimal amount of foreground when a full parking lot fronts the building. Also, owners may dampen sidewalks and parking lots with water to create a glistening surface that contrasts with and highlights the building's architecture. Plant abundant colorful flowers and, if possible, photograph during the spring or fall when fully leafed trees frame the property.

My company once acquired a building with an existing bank of photographs. The eight-story building stood adjacent to a main interstate freeway, with terrific commute access. When the aerial photographer shot the picture at 7 a.m. one Tuesday morning, a golden sunrise streamed light onto the building. Unfortunately, the photographer also managed to capture the snarled traffic from that morning's car accident. While there's a thin line between accuracy and misrepresentation, choosing to showcase a poor image seems foolish. The moral of the story: consider the story the photograph tells your prospective tenants.

Like people, some properties just don't photograph well. To compensate, consider shooting an interesting aspect of the property, like a corner balcony, which might serve as a metaphor for the entire building. Enlarged and artistically presented, such an architectural image, used independently or as a background screen with text, can create a quality advertisement. Another alternative is a colored sketch of the property. Renderings, however, can imply a building is in the design phase or under construction, so be aware that prospects may perceive it as a future—rather than a current—availability. With some creativity, any property can be represented by an image that attracts prospective tenants.

Finally, organize electronic and printed photographs for easy access. By separating and numbering the photographs by property, you will have a reference catalog that you can use for a variety of projects. Many leasing professionals slip the photograph into a plastic sheet protector and then label the folder.

IS THIS MY GOOD SIDE? ENSURE QUALITY PHOTOS

- ☐ Consider photographing in spring or fall, with fully leafed trees and flowers in bloom.
- ☐ Schedule the shoot for early morning or late afternoon for the best light.
- ☐ Wet the pavement in front of the building so it glistens.
- ☐ Ensure clean windows.
- ☐ Make sure the area is free of traffic, construction, dumpsters, delivery trucks, etc.
- ☐ Minimize the foreground if there's a large (asphalt) parking lot.
- ☐ Consider a close-up of an architectural feature or landscaping if the building doesn't photograph well.
- ☐ Obtain image copyrights from the photographer.

LOGOS

A logo achieves success when it is a recognizable symbol that communicates the landlord's values, such as quality, service, size, price, or convenience. Jacob Cass of Just Creative likes simple designs and says, "A refined and

> **Proud Owner of a Logo**
> Creating a logo for an individual building,
> especially one with significant available space,
> lends a sense of distinction to the project.

distilled identity will also catch the attention of a viewer."[5] Cass points to distinctive logos such as Nike's graphic swoosh or the McDonald's arches and notes their visual distinction even when "the subject matter of a logo is of relatively little importance."[6] Logos need versatility to be printed in one color, scaled larger and smaller, and printed in reverse (light logo on a dark background).

PAPER STOCK

Paper, also known as stock, is a critical ingredient in the printing process. The paper's weight and thickness drive cost, with typical bond weights between twenty pounds and thirty-two pounds, with twenty-four pounds being the most common for letterhead. Deeply saturated color requires stock on the heavier side. Photographs print best on white or ivory glossy paper, although be sure to use stock that resists fingerprint marks so multiple hands can collate a package without its appearing tattered. In addition, paper can connote sustainability through recycled materials, look, or texture. Paper with enough recycled content will be marked with the green recycling icon that appeals to an environmentally aware audience.

Content and Copy

WRITE STRONG COPY

When it comes to copy, conventional wisdom is best: keep it short and sweet. For brevity, a seventeen or so word limit per sentence or phrase works. And as for the sweet, put your best foot forward by listing the building's strongest attributes in bulleted form or in a succinct paragraph.

Because there's a difference between real estate clichés and effective messages, pay attention to word choice. Remember the high school English teacher who cringed at the passive verb *is*? Old Mrs. Murphy knew her stuff; active verbs make sentences sing. Common real estate nouns such as *view, remodel,* and *fitness center* can be amplified with verbs such as *"enjoys* panoramic views of downtown" or *"use* the twenty-four-hour fitness center."

Diction should include positive language. For example, "Fitness center membership included" sounds better than "Tenants don't have to pay for fitness center." Semantics, and their underlying attitudes, have a way of stretching their tentacles into every facet of a lease deal. By using positive statements, you create an encouraging tone for tenants and imbue the transaction with confidence.

I learned the power of proofreading the hard way when creating my first building flier. The flier included a map of the western United States, indicating the locations in which our company owned and managed property—six cities in all. After I opened the box containing freshly printed color fliers, I handed one to an office mate. He remarked wryly, "I didn't know Salt Lake City was in Nevada." What?! There it was, a geographical error, printed

*one thousand times over in glorious color. Although
I had reviewed the proof, seeing multiple versions
had blinded me to errors. I vowed to show any
future pieces to a panel of three discerning individuals. Mistakes happen, but a quality review can
preempt most of them.*

CRYSTALLIZE THE MESSAGE

Message clarity and consistency across media outlets create brand recognition, the public persona of a company.
While one might argue that a company such as Google
achieves better results with its whimsical daily animations,
even Google repeats its primary colors in a recognizable
font and uses an advertising-free opening page.

Further, realize that prospective tenants have relatively short-term exposure to the marketplace because
of the long-term nature of leases. Tenants may only truly
enter the market every three or five or even ten years,
which makes the sporadic messages they do hear more
important. So a property's message must communicate
the most significant features of the property whenever a
tenant engages in the market. By tweaking aspects of the
message but maintaining a basic script and look, landlords
can make their brands both recognizable and relevant. In
short, stay consistent, whether it's a logo, tagline, tweet,
mission statement, or design.

COMMUNICATE YOUR MISSION

A mission statement sums up a company's purpose in
words. Typically longer than a tagline, such statements

clarify a company's business goals and are included in annual reports, brochures, newsletters, and websites.

> *Fifteen years after my company's formation, our president hired a facilitator to help us craft a mission statement. I can't remember what prompted the drive to formalize the statement—perhaps a notion that we would someday become a public company—but I do remember thinking it unnecessary. After all, we were a profitable, growing company. Why did we need a mission statement?*
>
> *After the exercise, I did a 180-degree turnabout. While creating a mission statement did not change who we were, it did crystallize our purpose. With twelve or so executives gathered around a conference table, we talked about what was truly meaningful to our business. Repeated notions such as integrity, sustainable value, and relationships ultimately ended up in a statement that might do any real estate company proud:*

>> *Our mission is to provide productive work environments of sustainable value for our tenants and partners by creating timeless office projects managed with intense care. We diligently practice sound business principles and honor the integrity of our relationships as inviolate.*

CONSIDER ADDING A TAGLINE

A tagline expresses a company's mission and culture with a phrase or a few words. Examples include Nike's "Just Do

It" or 7Up's "The Uncola." Taglines often accompany a logo and are treated in a consistent manner in terms of font, color, and type.

Publishing and Printing

GRAPHIC DESIGNERS (AND COPYWRITERS)

Depending on your budget and the scope of design services you need to produce a marketing piece, you may decide to work with graphic designers and copywriters. While initial costs may be higher, designers can often save you money over the long haul because they produce artwork and copy that can be manipulated in a variety of ways. For example, a color logo must also be available in black and white (also called gray scale) for use when color isn't available or proves too costly. To have that option, you need a logo design that is as interesting in black and white as it is in color. Remember that, like the rest of our gig-job world, inexpensive online design resources abound, with companies that source freelance designers from all over the world.

The graphic designer can also act as a general contractor of sorts, responsible for oversight of a printing project in addition to the design. When selecting graphic designers, ask to review their design portfolios, which give examples of their styles and types of work. Once hired, such designers usually have established relationships with printers and will provide production specifications and obtain an estimate for the print job. Finally, remember to insist on a press check (the final review prior to printing) when signing the contract.

Copywriters often work in-house with a graphic designer (sometimes the same person) or come referred by the graphic designer. Excellent copywriters can distill culture and information into pithy sentences that communicate a property's offerings.

THE PRINTING HOUSE

For printing jobs, remember that size matters. The press-run size of a job remains its single largest cost component. These economies of scale mean that increased copies lower unit costs, with fewer setup resources needed for one large printing run than numerous small runs. As such, an accurate estimate of the number of advertising copies you'll need becomes critical. The adage "measure twice, cut once" is especially true when talking about printing jobs.

> **While yelling "Stop the presses!" makes for a dramatic movie moment, it's a very expensive phrase to shout in real life. So make sure you or someone with good visual sense and spelling skills (e.g., the graphic artist) attends the press check on your behalf.**

The All-Important Press Check

Usually held at the printing warehouse, the press check is your last chance to catch errors and ensure quality before the heavy printing equipment swings into full gear. While yelling "Stop the presses!" makes for a dramatic movie moment, it's a very expensive phrase to shout in real life. So make sure you or someone with good visual sense and spelling skills (e.g., the graphic artist) attends the press check on your behalf. You, the client, will also be asked to approve any final proof (or press check) prior to the production of marketing materials. Take your time to verify that each detail is accurate prior to approving the job.

DO IT YOURSELF (OR ALMOST) PUBLISHING

Sometimes a slim budget, a deadline, or the relatively good quality of office printers brings a printing job in-house. In the event you print your own materials or photographs, remember to play with the resolution to get a true idea of output quality. Also, you may need to adjust the color, as photographs appear lighter in print than they do on a computer monitor. And if you are working with an online service that will print materials (rather than a traditional printer's run), try to get a sample of the published product so you have the opportunity to proof and correct it prior to the completion of the entire job.

CHAPTER 4

Work with Brokers

"At the end of the day, I believe integrity
and relationships are everything in this business."[1]
—*Bill Wilson, founder, William Wilson & Associates*

GOAL: TO CULTIVATE STRONG
RELATIONSHIPS IN THE BROKERAGE
COMMUNITY

Leasing success, especially over the long term, depends on strong brokerage relationships. Whether you represent the landlord yourself or enlist others to provide those services, understanding a broker's role informs most lease deals. This chapter discusses how to understand, build, and maintain relationships with the brokerage community.

Recognize the Brokerage's Evolving Role

Ken Auletta, longtime columnist for the *New Yorker*, argues that technology, with its wealth of market information, threatens a broker's traditional role. Auletta cites the disappearance of superfluous middlemen who failed to couple content with service.[2] Successful real estate brokers must analyze data to create informed, fair deals for clients. In addition, clients require curated tours, proposal management, and documentation. Providing reassurance for some tenants and savvy negotiation for others, brokers employ a range of skills to procure the best deal for their clients.

Ironically, today's technology illuminates the benefits quality brokers can provide. With such a large amount of market data available, wouldn't those with industry experience provide valuable insight? Brokerages extol their ability to analyze—not just regurgitate—data. Moreover, experienced professionals bring a nuanced understanding of local markets.

Still, industry expectations can pressure brokers to justify their commission expense, sometimes creating tension in the deal. Professional landlords understand the dynamics that underpin commissions and often seek to strengthen relationships by appreciating brokers and creating a collaborative atmosphere through their communication and attitude.

As a leasing director and property manager, I sometimes had advance information that spaces might become available. I kept a log of brokers who were looking for certain types of spaces (for example, an office with a view or a 10,000 square foot already-constructed open plan) and might call to let them know of a pending opportunity. A personal shopper of sorts, I tried to add value by helping brokers source inventory and to minimize my own potential vacancy period. Shaving time from the leasing process becomes a boon to landlords eager to collect rent and to tenants anxious to occupy functional space.

Understanding Broker Roles

Although brokers may specialize in either tenant or land-lord representation, many brokers represent both (although not usually in the same deal). Here are some of the various roles played by brokers.

LISTING BROKER: THE LANDLORD'S REPRESENTATIVE

When a landlord employs a broker to represent a property in the marketplace, the broker becomes the *listing agent*

A Broker by Any Other Name

Listing brokers (who represent the landlord) are also known as *inside* or *in-house* brokers, and these terms are used interchangeably. On the other hand, procuring brokers (who represent the tenant) are known as *outside* or *tenant* or *cooperating* brokers. Listing brokers represent the lessor while procuring brokers represent the lessee.

and the contract is referred to as a *listing agreement*. A listing broker's duties include preparing a marketing plan, creating marketing collateral (brochures, fliers, etc.), hosting open houses, coordinating tours, analyzing financial statements, preparing proposals, and negotiating lease terms on behalf of the landlord. In addition, brokers educate landlords on local markets and keep them informed on the leasing progress. Listing brokers add value to these daily leasing tasks with their knowledge of the marketplace and professional relationships.

PROCURING BROKER: THE TENANT'S REPRESENTATIVE

On the other side of the equation, procuring brokers represent tenants in parallel aspects of their property searches, from market education to tours to lease negotiations.

With tenant representation, the extent of broker involvement varies depending on the tenant, the individual broker, and the landlord. For instance, if a broker has a national relationship with a substantially sized tenant, the broker may introduce the property and then let the

Opportunity Costs

Time and elbow grease play a role in any deal. Why negotiate with a difficult landlord who demands a fifty-page lease and takes weeks to respond when others answer immediately? Responsive, pleasant landlords often enjoy brokers flocking to their properties where they can get a deal done.

in-house tenant real estate team run with the deal. Other brokers will manage every detail of the leasing process. And still others, secure that the landlord will pay the broker a commission and play fair, feel comfortable letting the landlord and tenant reach a certain point in the process and then relinquishing some involvement (particularly when it's a landlord's existing tenant).

Understanding Brokerage Commissions

Lease commissions are the central financial incentive for brokers and are set by negotiations between brokers and landlords. As such, paying commissions commensurate with the marketplace becomes all-important, assuming you compete with other properties for tenants (and you don't have a monopoly or extremely special market niche).

Broker vs. Salesperson: What's the Diff?

While all states require that real estate sales professionals be licensed by that state, brokers are generally required to complete more education and have more experience than a salesperson. Real estate salespeople *hang* their licenses *under* the brokers' (a figurative, not literal term; although, a copy of the license must be retained in the office of employment). Commissions are remitted to the brokers who then pay the salespeople their portions.

Just as you educate yourself on local rents, you must know what commissions other landlords pay. Remember to include incentives that might augment the commission— speedier payments, bonus payments, and the occasional raffle ticket for a new car!

TYPICAL COMMISSION STRUCTURES

Commercial real estate brokerage commissions are typically based on a percentage of rent or a flat rate per square foot. Often remitted in two payments, the first half is usually paid upon lease signature and the second half upon lease commencement (often when the tenant takes occupancy of the space).

In a rent-based commission scenario, a broker is typically paid according to a percentage of the tenant's annual gross rent, with a declining percentage as the lease term progresses. For example, if a broker says "5-5-5-4-4," it means that the landlord pays a commission equal to 5 percent each of the tenant's first, second, and third years of rent and 4 percent each of the tenant's fourth and fifth years of rent. For longer-term leases, percentages likely extend to cover each year of rent, usually on a declining percentage basis. Many landlords like this arrangement because the commission remains somewhat tied to rental rates, so that a listing broker who negotiates a high rent reaps a benefit too.

Another common scenario is basing the commission on a flat rate per rentable square foot leased by the tenant. When speaking of this structure, for example, landlords will say the commission is $5 a foot. Thus, a 2,500 square foot suite would generate a commission of $12,500 ($5 multiplied by 2,500 square feet) for a five-year term. In the event of longer-term leases, such as seven- or ten-year lease terms, landlords may adjust the commission to $7 or $10 per square foot, respectively. Some landlords like this structure because of its straightforward calculation. Also, if the landlord offers a higher commission rate (via this square footage approach) than the percentage schedule allows, it can be simpler to communicate in advertisements.

Next, there's the issue of commission split, with a series of divisions. Typically, the listing broker's share of a lease commission depends on the involvement (or not) of a representing broker. For example, when a tenant comes directly to a building without a representing broker, the landlord's listing broker might earn the entire commission. However, if a representing—also known as the procuring or outside—broker brings the tenant, the landlord might pay a full commission to the procuring broker and then some additional amount (such as an extra half commission) to the landlord's representative. By offering a full commission to these outside brokers, there's little incentive for a broker to differentiate between buildings strictly on the basis of a commission.

Next in the series of splits, individual outside brokers must split their commissions with their employing brokerage companies. These splits are arranged internally between company and individual, commensurate with the salesperson's deal-making ability, experience, and so on. For example, newbie brokers might split their commissions fifty-fifty with their employing brokerage houses, while veteran rainmaker brokers might enjoy splits of 60 percent and higher. These internal company splits remain invisible to the landlord who pays the brokerage house. Whew, that sounds complicated, but keep plugging along, and you'll deepen your understanding of brokerage.

> ### Learn the Lingo
> In industry jargon, 5-5-5-4-4 means a commission equal to 5 percent of the annual rent for each of the first three years and 4 percent of the annual rent for each of the last two years of a five-year lease term.

PAYMENT

Payday! That sunny day when the celestial skies align and the lush golf course looms large. After the lease ink dries, landlords can expedite commission payments and deliver them to brokers. If presenting the check in person is not possible, write a note to accompany it. Even electronic transfers can be communicated to the broker with a telephone call or email. The point is to use the commission delivery to strengthen your brokerage relationships, rather than settle for a perfunctory payment that arrives in a stack of mail.

On a logistical note, in-person commission delivery may entail coordinating with your accountant so that you

> ### Bang for the Buck
> Some landlords expedite commission payments and deliver them to the broker over lunch. The personal touch lets a broker know that you value the relationship.

receive the check rather than it being delivered directly to the brokerage house. Although it's a little hassle, the pay-offs of a better brokerage relationship are huge. And you avoid that awkward telephone call from the broker asking for payment and tainting the deal experience with administrative bother.

A brief note should accompany the second half of the commission payment too (usually when the tenant moves into the space). The payment reminds the broker of your property months after the deal's conclusion. If any of your interactions with the broker have become confrontational during the course of the deal, redeem yourself with an in-person commission delivery.

> *I came to appreciate the tough realities of a commission-based job when an older broker called me to pick up his commission check. The gracious broker mentioned that he'd be in the area ... and drove the half hour from San Francisco's financial district to our offices. I doubt he wanted to visit the suburbs; more likely, he needed the cash. That incident made me consider the uneven stream of income for brokers, particularly in down markets. Since then, I expedite the commission checks through accounting, tell the brokers when the checks will be ready, and when possible, deliver them myself. It's extra work, but the resulting positive relationships are priceless.*

Building Relationships with the Brokerage Community

A WORD ON CULTURE

Real estate is a relationship-based culture and attracts extroverted, charismatic people. Examples include Roger Staubach, Heisman Trophy winner, Super Bowl champion, and founder of his eponymous commercial real estate firm. While few of us are celebrated athletes, you can cultivate your own style of interaction with others.

Real Estate: An Industry That Loves a Good Acronym

BOMA: Building Owners and Managers Association (offers the Real Property Administrator designation)

CCIM: Certified Commercial Investment Member

CREW: Commercial Real Estate Women

IREM: Institute of Real Estate Management (offers the Certified Property Manager designation)

NAIOPL: Commercial Real Estate Development Associations

NAR: National Association of Realtors

SIOR: Society of Industrial and Office Realtors

ULI: Urban Land Institute

USGBC: United States Green Building Council (offers Leadership in Energy and Environmental Design designation)

I once heard about the managing partner of a law firm, a consultant to renowned companies, who returned every phone call within twenty-four hours. I resolved to do the same. Some crazy days, that meant I dashed off an email saying I'd received the message and would respond the following day (or at a named future date). I found brokers (and tenants) flocking to do business with our office, perhaps in part because of this responsive service.

The commercial real estate industry offers numerous communities for education, collaboration, and contribution. By joining one (or more) groups, many of which offer a professional designation, you deepen your industry knowledge and build relationships.

TRUST AND ATTITUDE

While leasing mechanics are important, it's the softer attribute of trust that makes a relationship work. Put bluntly, your integrity matters most. Should you treat someone unfairly, expect to be cocktail conversation for a long time thanks to real estate's robust grapevine.

As it happens, chemistry might inform both our trustworthiness as well as our instincts to trust others. Paul Zak, author of *The Moral Molecule*, indicates that the chemical oxytocin may play a significant role in why some people are trustworthy and others are not. Chemicals aside, Zak's studies also imply that actions can trigger behavioral responses. Zak explains that it's "another way of saying that the feeling of being trusted makes a person more . . . trustworthy."[3] The bottom line? Treat others as worthy peers and you may engender the same behavior in return.

> **"The feeling of being trusted makes a person more . . . trustworthy," says researcher Paul Zak.**

When applied to real estate, an intuitive leasing person appraises the breadth and strength of a broker's influence in every deal. A broker with whom you've completed many deals will usually cast your property in a favorable light. In contrast, other brokers may simply shop the market, presenting your property as an undistinguished option. Regardless, treat every broker with respect, even when you sense the tour might be an exercise in market education rather than authentic interest in your property.

MARKET INFORMATION: A DELICATE DIALOGUE

Market information, arguably a broker's greatest resource, constantly permeates the real estate community. By building strong broker relationships, you avail yourself of the type of factual deal data that allows your available space to

---

Swipe Right for a Hot Property

Some brokers use mobile devices to display floor plans, photographs, and building information, all of which can augment a tour. Make sure your local brokers have accurate information along with the best photos of your property by updating online listings regularly.

be most competitive and makes you knowledgeable about the industry.

Brokers and landlords use comparable information to justify rental (and other deal) numbers to owners, prospective clients, and other brokers. It's the analysis of such data, however, that adds real value and nuance. The evidence contained in signed leases provides the support for your leasing proposals and the ensuing negotiations.

Exchanging lease comparables presents a classic dilemma of wanting information without giving away the house. While this topic has been discussed earlier, the subject is worth revisiting. Real estate professionals can become tight-lipped when information gives them a competitive edge. While comparable information can be exchanged in nearly every interaction with a broker, it's usually woven into informal conversation. This type of casual exchange also requires an underlying vocabulary of real estate terms and market information from the participants.

It's a bit of an art to learn to trade information in a conversational way. As an example, an exchange might be as casual as this sample script:

> **Property manager:** "Congrats on the XYZ lease."
> **Outside broker:** "Thanks, it was a bear."
> **Property manager:** "I heard. Did they end up committing to seven years or ten?" (Specific question shows that the property manager knows something about the term and makes it easier to extract the answer.)
> **Outside broker:** "Ten, although they have an option to cancel after seven."

Of course, the above exchange is a typical example of how leasing personnel fill in the missing pieces of their knowledge to build a comprehensive understanding of the marketplace. Here's another sample:

> **Broker:** "Did you hear X Company has committed to the top floor of New Tower?"
> **Landlord rep:** "Have they topped off the building?" (Rep is asking if construction is nearing completion, which will lead to a tenant occupancy date. Since the landlord rep has researched the market, the rep knows the floor plate of New Tower measures 20,000 square feet, so the suite size is a known variable.)
> **Broker:** "Not yet."
> **Landlord rep:** "Well, hopefully we're on the invite list for the topping-off party!"

At this point the real estate professionals might move onto another topic and maintain an easy banter or they might delve deeper into talks about New Tower. Make sure you scribble some notes as soon as possible and enter them into your information database later.

As a note, occasionally a tenant or another party in a lease transaction will request a confidentiality agreement with respect to the terms of the lease transaction. Respect this, and move on to another topic. (Be aware that some professionals might insinuate such a confidentiality request—even sans a formal agreement—in order to refrain from sharing details that might hurt their own leasing efforts.)

Entertaining, Corporate Style

Whether at a white-tablecloth dinner or ballpark suite, most landlords cultivate relationships using social events that extend beyond the workday. Uptown or downtown, successful events share some attributes that get the most bang for your entertaining buck. So learning some entertaining basics can come in handy.

THE PURPOSE

What's the point of the event? Knowing your purpose allows you to tailor the social activities for maximum impact. Is it to attract brokers to available space? Highlight a renovation? Cultivate colleagues who can talk shop? Identifying what you want to achieve as well as what attendees will gain creates the framework for a successful event as details from decor to food can be assessed in terms of the end goal.

My firm hosted an annual Dealmaker's Dinner to honor brokers (plus their guests) whose clients had signed a lease with us that year. Each December, we booked a hot restaurant in San Francisco. The changing venue added a spark, as dining at the latest Michelin star restaurant seemed akin to a lottery win. We hired limos to transport guests. At the dinner, we acknowledged Repeat Offenders, brokers who'd completed more than one deal in that year or previous years, with a special gift. The event became a coveted invitation—a fun, luxurious, and exclusive evening that built friendships. With over 80 percent of invitees saying yes to the invitation, it proved a hit.

Branding

From the invitation to a promotional gift, each facet of the event offers a chance to convey mood and create consistency. Choose colors, fonts, and themes accordingly.

THE VENUE

Real estate professionals pay attention to physical space and the experience it generates. Evaluate the sound system, table layout, and seating arrangements. For tables, consider smaller tables (sixty-inch round or smaller) that create energy through physical proximity and conversation. While large or long tables may look stately, they often isolate guests by limiting conversation partners. For any gathering over eight people, assigned seating arrangements are a great idea. And remember that no one likes the dark table squeezed next to the swinging kitchen door.

In terms of sound, ensure that conversation and any speakers can be heard over ambient noise. It's anticlimactic to ask your dinner partner to repeat a joke's punch line. By previewing the sound system, you can ensure that the new analyst seated at the back of the restaurant can hear as well as the executive vice president at the table in the front.

One of the best and most cost-effective marketing events I held was a monthly Breakfast Club in various vacant office suites. We'd set up two or three tables; one with a buffet of coffee, tea, scrambled eggs, toast, made-to-order omelets, and lattes, and set the other table(s) for seated guests. Breakfast started at eight, and we'd welcome brokers, give a brief overview of the vacant space, throw out an interesting topic of the day, and eat. By nine, most brokers had departed. The casual, consistent nature of the event made organizing easy, costs reasonable, and the vacant space showcase effective. After all, everyone needs breakfast, right?

Restaurants and Caterers

There's a certain balance to selecting an interesting menu that kitchen staff can deliver on time and within budget. Corporate planners satisfy these sometimes-competing demands by combining standard menu items with customized choices. For example, you might serve the same appetizers, salad course, and dessert to everyone yet present two or three choices for the entrée. Limited choices appeal to the serving staff and usually create a better guest experience. After all, no one wants to watch their steaks cool while others wait for their salmon. Finally, verify that adequate staffing is included in the food contract. Include a server who greets guests with a tray of sparkling water and wine to kick-start the party. First impressions count, and it sure beats a long line at the bar.

Print the menu on the same paper and with the same theme as the invitation and place a copy at each table setting (wait until the day of the event to print the menus in

---

Make Alice Waters Proud

Remember that people attend events for an experience. Go long on excellent seasonal food and skip the predictable chicken entrées and ubiquitous cold custard fruit tart.

case of changes to the meal ingredients, and pending a final attendance count).

> *Remember bad Uncle Billy, the loud uncle who drank way too much before Thanksgiving dinner? Yes, we all have one. When I host a company event, I keep Billy in mind by limiting cocktails to an hour or less. Also, I make sure that servers pass bite-sized hors d'oeuvres (with cocktail napkins) so that guests can enjoy each other rather than push their way to a crowded table for a cracker. Parties are all about momentum, and if Uncle Billy doesn't eat anything, things spiral downward pretty quickly.*

LOGISTICAL PLANNING

Thinking through logistics that impact venue, budget, and most importantly, the guest experience is a critical, if less glamorous, part of event planning. Start by mentally walking through the event, beginning to end. Then, talk to the appropriate contacts (such as the caterer, valet, etc.) and resolve any outstanding items.

THE DEVIL IN THE LOGISTICAL DETAILS

- ☐ Parking, valet (and transportation)
- ☐ Lighting
- ☐ Sound system and acoustics
- ☐ Necessary bar and catering staff
- ☐ Seating arrangements
- ☐ Coat check
- ☐ Menu (and alternatives for those with allergies or other preferences)

☐ Alcoholic and nonalcoholic drinks

☐ Agenda and timing

BUDGETS

Corporate events reflect the current economy. In volatile markets, subdued gatherings rule the day, small in scale with targeted audiences. In bullish markets, anything goes. No really, it's real estate. Solid relationships, however, can be built with relatively modest events.

The event menu, bar, and labor drive the bulk of expenses. The menu cost depends on the ingredients, so many hosts temper a pricier item such as steak with a lower cost pasta or risotto. For drinks, event coordinators purchase wine separately and ask if the restaurant will provide corkage. Remember to negotiate wine prices as restaurants usually quote on a per-bottle basis, and you will purchase in quantity. Timing plays into the budget, too, as restaurants and caterers are often less expensive and more flexible on weekdays.

Tips for the Budget Conscious

- Hold the event on a weekday—restaurants and associated costs rise on the weekend.
- Breakfast and lunch are less expensive than dinner.
- Offer poured glasses of wine and water instead of a full bar.

TIMING

When scheduling any event, consider the audience and the type of event. For example, a Friday evening without spouses, partners, or guests can prove disastrous as people race to weekend plans. And meetings or emergencies can fill Mondays. Event planners often choose Thursdays for lunch or dinner. Guests are a little more relaxed as the week winds on, yet the event doesn't interfere as much with personal time.

THE GUEST LIST

When it comes to corporate events, a curated guest list produces the best results. Have a specific reason to offer a spot to each invitee and then do everything possible to create an invitation and event that will elicit positive attendance from that group.

Piggybacking

Companies capitalize on large glitzy events by arranging smaller exclusive gatherings around the larger one. For example, take advantage of companies on location at a convention, without incurring the cost of transportation or significant coordination, by hosting a small cocktail reception in a private suite before the keynote speech.

One of our company executives enjoyed inviting couples to dinner. His rationale: meeting a spouse or partner allows you to know your guest in a more authentic manner. Although perhaps a bit mercenary, the executive also believed that individuals would act with more integrity once he had been introduced to their inner circles.

Invitations

Good invitations generate excitement, especially when great restaurants, popular music, and hard-to-secure tickets are involved. In terms of the actual invitation, David Eiland, president and co-owner of San Francisco's Just for Fun, says successful hosts "make the invitation speak to the event."[4] Eiland suggests unique invitations that don't disappear under last week's utility bill. For example, a paneled card that displays construction elements (hard-hat, shovel) with an inserted nut and bolt at the top of the invitation might celebrate a construction groundbreaking. Another client uses easel-backed invitations for vertical display atop a desk. Keep your budget in mind, though; $5 or less per invitation set is a good rule.

Your invitation should generate event buzz by showcasing a fun venue, notable guests, interesting speakers, or a great activity. Make sure the invitation speaks to (i.e., is consistent with) the event. As with all communication, pay extra attention to names: Bill Smith likely won't open an envelope addressed to "W.R. Smithe" because of the misspelling and unlikely use of initials.

Social Secretary

When inviting a significant number of guests from one company, verify the date with that business's office manager for potential conflicts.

ENVELOPES SHOULD BE:

- ☐ Personally addressed, not labeled
- ☐ Stamped, not metered (commemorative stamps are even better)
- ☐ Properly stuffed (so the invitation is face up when one opens the envelope)

RSVPs

Receiving accurate responses from invited guests starts with a complete invitation (who, what, where, when, why). For instance, invitations should list a telephone number or email along with the contact's name and a specific due date for responses. On the host's side, the RSVP contact person needs all the event information to answer any questions. Once past the indicated response date, you'll likely need to follow up with stragglers to make sure they received an invitation and to see if they can attend. And please, avoid the dreaded "Regrets only," which generates poor response and leaves you in the dark for planning. Keep a spreadsheet of responses that lists the attendee's name, company, address, telephone number, guest name (if applicable), RSVP of yes or no, and any other applicable columns (table number, golf index, etc.). Some event organizers use an

Gauging the Turnout

FORMAL FUNCTIONS: Turnout rates of 60–65 percent are excellent.
CASUAL EVENTS: Expect a 35–50 percent positive response.
NO-SHOWS: Anticipate 8–10 percent and plan accordingly. Have an alternative seating plan so guests have company and servers can quickly whisk away the extra setting.

extra column to itemize information such as allergies, likes/dislikes, and so on.

THE ACTUAL EVENT

When the event starts, welcome guests at the door and greet them by name. Have fun, but not too much fun—remember you're the host. Be true to your invitation. If you invited guests to a dinner, don't talk shop over dessert. Instead, ask about their children, a recent trip, or a hobby. As the venerable Emily Post writes, "Good manners are, after all, nothing but courteous consideration of other people's interests and feelings."[5] The goal is to build connections with others by getting to know them and making them comfortable.

For one client event, we hired a stand-up comic who started with a couple of unimpressive magic tricks. Next, he picked an audience member to embarrass. Too bad it was a senior VP who'd flown in from New York and didn't take kindly to being the butt of the joke. The room fell quiet, and I wished for a giant hook to yank him offstage. That cringeworthy moment taught me to preview any entertainer— musician, magician, or comic—before booking.

FOLLOW-UP

A brief "Thanks for coming" note or photo mailed after the event provides another touchstone for relationships. Posting photographs online to memorialize the event might be expedient, but be sure that posted items remain business appropriate. Remember, it's all about the relationship.

Promotional Gifts

Promotional gifts are part of a well-designed marketing package as they advertise your company and remind others of a relationship, long after the party lights fade. According to the Promotional Products Association International, the challenge is to relate promotional products to the recipient. More often than not, that means appealing to the so-called millennial who comprises the largest share of the US workforce (one in three professionals) and who values purpose, access to assets, and engaging experiences.[6] While some groups donate to a favorite nonprofit, other hosts look to trends in the retail marketplace for relevant gifts. For timing, four weeks lead time is ideal for product conception, production, and delivery.

From cool outdoorsy jackets to the latest tech gadget, businesses tout symbols that connote status and success. Consider the canvas duffel bags first made popular by EF Hutton and carried by investment bankers, slung across their chests, a cross between county club and hip messenger bag. It became a symbol of a good education and a good job. While the gifts may change, the message stays the same— that of success.

PART II

Structuring the Lease Deal

CHAPTER 5

Tour Prospective Tenants

"I'm convinced that buyers decide if they're going to buy your house within the first eight seconds of seeing it. So set your stopwatch, get out of your car, and see what you see in the first eight seconds."[1]
—*Barbara Corcoran, founder, The Corcoran Group*

> **GOAL:** GIVE A TOUR THAT WILL LAND YOUR BUILDING ON THE PROSPECTIVE TENANT'S COVETED SHORTLIST

Three figures stumble along a dimly lit corridor. The woman in the navy blazer works the key into a stubborn lock and pushes against the scratched door. Inside the musty office, her hand fumbles for the light switch. Finally, lights flicker on to reveal a space whose blinds are shut tight against the afternoon sun. The tour, the tour, the classic tour.

The tour is our brief moment on stage, a chance to meet face to face with the tenants and show the best parts of our property and how it might fit their needs. In some ways, the tour serves as the most acute test of the market as tenants decide whether or not to pursue space in a specific building. Importantly, the meeting allows a personal connection between the landlord and the prospective tenant, a sizing-up of a potential relationship. Tenants will assess your integrity and professionalism, which will affect their experience as a building occupant. At the same time, leasing agents will try to get a sense of tenants and their business. Tours either spark the embers for a long-term business relationship or douse the flame.

And it all happens so fast. Studies show that first impressions—or rapid cognition—occur within seconds. Coined *thin slicing*, the psychological term refers to a human's ability to make sense of situations quickly.[2] The theory that humans make judgments in astonishingly brief periods of time and then use the balance of their time to justify their initial thoughts underscores the importance of curb appeal. Long-term leasing decisions may hinge on our prospect's first view of a property's parking lot or on our own introductions. Part rigorous preparation, part show, part intuition, tours are an artful science that you cultivate with practice.

Arrange the Tour

HANDLE INITIAL INQUIRIES

Most tours start days or weeks before a visit, with a telephone call. While brokers and prospective tenants both research properties online, brokers will usually also call landlords to confirm and discuss space availability. Uninterested brokers rarely waste time with this type of telephone call (unless they represent one of your existing tenants and are scouting for information), so treat each call as a bona fide prospect.

In order to organize these inquiries, leasing professionals use a software program, an electronic spreadsheet, or go old school with paper to log the inquiry. As you speak with brokers, note their names and contact information, the tenant's size requirement, and if a broker will convey it, the tenant's name and current office location. If the broker does not book a tour in the following couple of days, add this broker to your weekly (or biweekly) call list to see if the tenant is still a prospect. If the tenant has pursued another building, stay in touch with the broker. Sometimes deals fall apart and prospective tenants are back in the market, searching for space. In addition, tracking the inquiry (and ultimate deal comps) allows you to round out your market information.

The more specific the broker or prospect is about a space requirement, the greater the chance the prospect is legitimate. For example, if the broker conveys the square footage, provides the tenant's name and business, states any other requirements (looking for ample parking, signage a must, etc.) and most importantly, gives a compelling reason for the tenant to leave its existing building, the prospect appears viable.

If a broker, however, will not divulge much information, consider one of the following possibilities. First, the broker may not have control of the tenant, meaning that he may not have obtained an exclusive listing agreement to provide tenant representation. Second, the broker might be trying to represent your own existing tenant. By asking about availability, particularly in the tenant's size range, the broker feels out a potential rent renewal (and possible leasing commission). And third, the broker might have control of the tenant, but the tenant does not want the marketplace to know it's looking for space—perhaps the tenant is high profile, or is trying to negotiate with its current landlord, or wants to keep information (such as a company downsizing) confidential.

Meeting prospective tenants will provide more information to ascertain their true intentions. At any rate, be aware of the above possibilities so as not to cannibalize your own leasing efforts. This awareness requires somewhat of a double-faced attitude. On one hand, you must treat the inquiry as a straightforward opportunity to lease space to a new tenant. On the other hand, as a landlord, you are trying to hedge against losing an existing tenant or complicating a lease renewal with an existing tenant.

SCHEDULE THE TOUR

Given an opportunity, leasing representatives can improve tours with some attention to timing. For instance, ask for the first or last slot on a tour itinerary to allow your property to emerge from the crowd. One caveat—avoid the slot right before lunch, because hunger tends to cloud judgment. As evidence, one university study evaluated nearly a thousand judicial rulings over a ten-month period and discovered that the highest percentage of prisoners given parole occurred after breakfast (65%) and lunch (70%). The percentage of prisoners given parole immediately before lunch shriveled to nearly zero.[3] While you can't compare prospective tenants to prisoners, you might schedule tours in the morning or early afternoon if possible, before hunger pangs overwhelm everyone.

Talking Rent Before the Tour

For tour purposes, it is best to talk in generalities and quote a range of rents. Hear what the broker thinks is a comparable, and if it's incorrect (and accrues to your advantage), correct any inaccuracies.

Next, limit the number of tour suites at any one property to a maximum of three. For laypeople, buildings and suites can become a jumbled blur as they learn about neighborhoods, properties, and specific spaces. Start with the suite you believe is most appealing. Even if the tenants find that suite not quite to their liking, the positive attributes of an appealing suite can carry over to another, more appropriate space at the same property.

BE AWARE OF EXISTING SPACE ENCUMBRANCES

Before showing vacant space, make sure you understand any encumbrances on the suite—that is, the rights other existing tenants have with regard to that space. To help keep records straight, colored floor plans or lease software helps track rights. (Because granting tenants rights creates a complex puzzle to manage, experienced leasing agents become parsimonious when negotiating such concessions, but more on that later.)

In the event of encumbrances on a particular space you plan to show, make sure to communicate the proper notices. For example, if an existing tenant has a right of first offer, send the notifying letter before showing the vacant space. If there's a right of first refusal or other expansion right that hinges on another interested third party, disclose such to your prospective tenant at an appropriate time so you can administer the existing lease agreement properly and your prospect isn't furious. These notices—usually a letter—generally require a specific format to ensure they comply with the terms of the lease, so make sure your legal counsel approves the letter.

CHECKLIST OF COMMON ENCUMBRANCES

- ☐ Right of first (or second or third) offer
- ☐ Right of first (or second or third) refusal
- ☐ Right of lease extension
- ☐ Right of expansion
- ☐ Right of termination
- ☐ Right of relocation

Make the Space Appealing

Studying individual spaces, with their attributes and challenges, allows you to craft customized marketing plans and presentations that lead to better leasing results.

Effective leasing agents take oldie-but-goodie songwriter Johnny Mercer's advice to "accentuate the positive, eliminate the negative," especially relative to competing buildings.[4] Calling attention to positive attributes, via marketing materials and in presentations, keeps the property's best characteristics front and center in the prospective tenant's mind.

I know a developer who assesses buildings with a quick peek into the stairwell. If the stairwell is swept clean and well lit, he knows the property maintenance staff is top notch. Why? He reasons that only high-quality real estate personnel pay attention to the spaces rarely seen. Conversely, if stairwell lights are burned out or cigarettes clutter the corners, he's found a mediocre manager and an owner that does not care about details (Caution: if you try this yourself and the stairwell door closes behind you, be prepared to walk all the way down the flights to the building exit! Fire codes can require locked doors to preserve the fire-rating function of a stairwell.)

ACCENTUATE THE POSITIVE

To promote a property, focus on its three most appealing qualities. The time-honored selling points for real estate remain constant: location, access, cost, amenities, and quality of space. While these traditional values point you in the right direction, evaluate your own property for its strongest assets.

In addition, the most desirable space mirrors the cultural values now prevalent in today's society, with emphasis on flexibility, technology, and health. Yesterday's paneled corner office has given way to today's bright open-plan offices where hoodie-clad CEOs share stand-up desks alongside employees. Technology companies and their offices provide the archetype of today's equalitarian business ethos. For instance, author Ken Auletta explains that Google founders wanted "to recreate the feel of the Stanford [University] campus" where employees could gather each Friday afternoon for nachos, hamburgers, and drinks, "with employees at other Google locations around the world on videoconference."[5] While not every tenant

Living Green

Studies support the notion that optimal office space promotes productivity and reduces employee absenteeism. Chicago-area researcher and consultant Tim Springer, PhD, lists important design criteria as: spatial equity (adequate privacy, daylight, and access to views for all), healthfulness (free of harmful contaminants and excessive noise), flexibility for easy configuration, comfort, technological connectivity, reliability, and a sense of space.[6]

shares this culture, Google's example reflects marketplace trends of informality and technological connectedness. Undoubtedly, space preferences will change over time, but understanding trends allows you to make your tours relevant.

When assessing space, pay attention to details that promote any of the attributes valued in your marketplace. For example, good lighting and the ability for individuals to adjust room temperature create an enjoyable environment. While unique characteristics such as exposed brick or high ceilings are evident during tours, health features such as carpets that contain a minimal amount of chemicals need to be proactively highlighted. As you assess your space, note these items so you can incorporate them into your tour presentation.

Wise leasing agents weave building assets into a consistent tour itinerary. For instance, if your building boasts views, consider starting your tours from a great vantage point and then reiterate the view via high-quality photographs (of the same) throughout the floor lobbies. Or, if your building has an excellent café or gourmet coffee kiosk, you can greet brokers or prospective tenants with a prettily wrapped baked good or to-go coffee and mention the café's quality. Some building owners dedicate a parking space for prospects to guarantee smooth tour arrivals. The point is to show, rather than just tell, the best parts of the building. In addition to physical space, landlords can distinguish themselves with excellent service. This attribute remains very much within your control and can be a game changer for prospective tenants. For instance, a leasing agent who introduces a uniformed engineer or friendly concierge or relates a story about staff service underscores the landlord's quality. Although service remains a soft feature of the property as opposed to architectural features or engineering aspects, it's a significant element of any building. Perhaps the conventional saying that real estate is all about "location, location, location" should be changed to "location, service, service." Excellent property management can best a competing building that lacks attentive care for its occupants because it's particularly important in a long-term relationship.

Because I managed a small building that couldn't afford a full-time concierge, I subcontracted an online concierge service. The nominal fee was billed back to the tenants via operating expenses. The virtual concierge could secure tickets to events, make travel reservations, and complete local errands at a fraction of the cost of employing an individual to do the same. My tenants loved the extra help a keyboard click away.

ELIMINATE THE NEGATIVE

To preview a property from the perspective of your prospects, take a walk in their shoes. Arrive at the property as if you are a first-time visitor. Notice that crowded parking lot? That stained or worn carpet? That dark suite? Each fleeting experience informs a prospective tenant about a landlord's attention to maintenance and property management service.

Once you've arrived at the vacant (or soon to be vacant) suite, make a list of the needed maintenance items. Be sure to eliminate all signs of previous tenancy—everyone likes fresh, new spaces. For improvements such as new paint, select a neutral color for long-term value. Once you've completed the cleanup or improvements to the vacant suite, place it on a regular janitorial schedule to ensure maintenance.

Next, assess any leasing challenges and brainstorm potential (or partial) solutions. For example, is the suite situated down a long hallway? It may be best to meet the broker and prospective tenant in the building lobby rather than trekking down a corridor to the management office and then backtracking to the suite. This approach de-emphasizes the corridor length and gives the tenant a realistic sense of the path to the proposed suite.

Another challenging instance may be a suite with a sweeping view . . . of the parking lot. Some attractive (evergreen rather than deciduous) trees or shrubs planted outside the office windows will soften the outlook. In this situation, open—but do not raise—the blinds for increased light. Turn lemons into lemonade by marketing the suite to a sales firm or to companies with frequent visitors, where parking lot proximity is an asset.

I once leased a mid-rise building with skimpy bay depths (the distance from the common corridor to the window line) of only twenty-three feet. Tenants struggled to visualize an office layout as they stepped into the narrow gray shell space. So I enlisted an architect to sketch potential office configurations. I then had the plans enlarged and displayed on foam board and easels. By anticipating questions and providing solutions with easy visuals, I was able to show tenants how the space might work for them.

GETTING PHYSICAL: PRIOR TO A TOUR

☐ Do the lights work?

☐ Do all the (squeak-free) doors open easily?

☐ Does the suite need recarpeting or carpet cleaning (furniture indentation marks removed)?

☐ Does the suite need repainting?

☐ Are the blinds open?

☐ Has the previous tenant's nameplate been removed from the front door?

☐ Are there other reminders of the previous tenant that need removal (kitchen debris, junk mail stuffed under the door)?

☐ Has the suite been placed on a janitorial maintenance schedule?

☐ Does the suite need some type of illustration of a potential configuration?

The Tour Presentation

Crafting a tour presentation allows you to present the property in its best light, makes good use of limited time, and frees your resources to focus on individual prospects.

While the term *script* may seem contrived, the best public speakers—and make no mistake, this is public speaking—prepare a delivery, even if it appears improvised. After all, why reinvent the wheel for each tour? Also, a crafted presentation makes the best use of limited tour time. Most brokers and prospective tenants allot twenty to forty-five minutes per building tour, and less if the tour does not capture their fancy. What good is a great selling point when watching the rear taillights of a prospect? Most importantly, because you know how you are going to present the property, you can pay attention to each prospect and tailor your delivery to their specific concerns.

BE BRIEF, BE POSITIVE

So, how to craft an effective tour? First, think brevity. A good introduction should last two minutes or less, especially given the brief nature of most broker visits. Add that to a prospect's dizzying schedule of multiple property tours and real estate jargon, and it's the perfect storm: glazed eyes, restless tenants, and impatient brokers. To stay relevant, make the introductory presentation short and crisp.

As a general note, use vocabulary that frames statements in a positive manner because optimism lends a forward motion to leasing. For example, when tenants ask if they might have a $50 per square foot improvement allowance, instead of replying "no," you might explain, "We give a competitive tenant improvement allowance of $25 per square foot and will work with you to achieve the most value for your tenant improvement dollar." This habit of framing questions with a positive response becomes important as you field questions from the prospect on the tour (more examples below).

I sell in a positive way and resist any temptation to speak negatively against competition. As an example, we successfully lobbied our city to install a left-hand turn signal into our parking lot. My competitor's building across the street, however, has a cumbersome U-turn a block away. So when highlighting access to the freeway, I point out that my property enjoys easy parking lot access via a turn signal that holds traffic at bay (especially helpful to a sales force that spends time in the car). I find little need to say anything negative about another property. By drawing attention to the positive aspects of my property, such comparisons are effectively made.

PREPARING A ROCK STAR PRESENTATION:

- ☐ What are the three best attributes of my property?
- ☐ How can I highlight these?
- ☐ What are the negative aspects of my property and can they be mitigated?
- ☐ Is my presentation brief and compelling enough (two minutes or under) to retain attention?

USE VISUAL AIDS

Next, think visually. Plan to start your property overview with an aerial photograph of the property, which can be displayed on an easel or carried to a tour group, if needed. Orient tour attendees to the property by noting the surrounding freeways (good access), available parking (if it is an amenity), and the front entrance of the building. While enumerating the various nearby amenities such as banks, restaurants, and shopping centers, plan to point to the locations on the photo. Then, use language that circles back to the building, noting some of the most prominent, long-standing tenants (it's cachet for you and shows you maintain good relationships). Consider finishing the overview with a story of a thriving tenant who has expanded in the building over time, to show your value as a long-term, quality landlord.

A Parting Package

At the close of the tour, plan to present the tenant with your (take-home) marketing package, which should include a floor plan, a color flier of the property and its attributes, an aerial photo if possible, an amenities list, and so on, all housed within a folder embossed or labeled with the building's name and logo. Many agents prefer this timing to avoid detracting from the oral presentation. (Refer to chapter 3 for more information about each of the marketing pieces.)

TRY ROLE-PLAYING

Practice your tour presentation by role-playing. First, rehearse your tour script in front of a mirror. Learn how to tailor the description and highlight items of interest for a particular prospective tenant. Then, give a sample tour to some colleagues and ask for a critique. Tell your colleagues that this first run through will likely be lousy; that way, they feel freer to give honest feedback rather than worry about crushing your psyche. Then, check your ego! Additionally, find someone who excels at leasing and shadow them giving a tour of your building. There's a confidence that comes from being the expert in the room, and you have the means to know more about your building or property than anyone else on the tour. So study your property, practice responses, and enjoy the feeling that comes with mastery.

SAMPLE SCRIPT FOR A PROPERTY OVERVIEW AND INTRODUCTION

(Point to locations on the aerial photo as appropriate.)

"To give you an overview, this is Cardinal Office Center, nestled with terrific access between Interstate 280 and Highway 101 alongside Highway 380, which connects the two. These two freeways serve as the major transit paths connecting San Francisco to the north with San Jose to the south. Cardinal Office Center offers seven buildings with nearly a million square feet of office space. Some of our long-term tenants include Fortune 500 Company A, Notable Technology Company B and International Firm C (tailor this list to the prospective tenant's business). We pride ourselves on offering tenants a high level of service and maintaining long-term working partnerships." (A note of caution here: know your audience. You don't want to inadvertently tell your prospect that a competing company occupies an office adjacent to the suite you plan to tour! Switch suites if possible).

"Some of the property amenities include a fitness center free to tenants within this building (point to map), the Convenient Shopping Center (point) with a grocery store, deli, post office and several small shops, and XYZ Bank. There are three restaurants within walking distance—ABC Deli, ABC Restaurant, and 123 Restaurant. We also offer an on-site conference center for tenants, which can be reserved through the management office."

"Let's go take a look at the suites we have available for you."

PREPARE FOR LIKELY QUESTIONS

Once you can deliver a smooth presentation, work on addressing common questions or concerns that arise during the course of a tour. Drill yourself on your own property knowledge by making a list of potential questions a tenant or broker might ask. The challenge is to answer questions in a positive manner. For example, if you only offer exterior monument signs to tenants leasing over 10,000 square feet, do not simply say no to a tenant requesting 1,500 square feet. Instead, present an alternative, such as, "You'll have signage on the main lobby directory and on your suite door on move-in day. We generally grant exterior signage rights for companies over 10,000 square feet. At the rate your company is growing, I expect you'll have a space that large in a few years." This ability to deliver a practiced presentation and answer impromptu questions results in a top-notch tour.

SOME TYPICAL QUESTIONS AND SAMPLE ANSWERS

Question: How much parking will I get?
Poor answer: Your company will only get three spaces.
Better answer: We grant parking on a ratio based on square footage leased; at this property, it is three spaces for every 1,000 square feet of space.

Question: What if my company needs to expand?

Poor answer: We hope we have space for you.

Better answer: That's a challenge we love to have. We have many examples of long-term tenants that have expanded over time. For instance, ABC Company initially leased 5,000 square feet, grew to 8,000 square feet, and just recently expanded its sales force and is now a 15,000 square foot tenant that has been here eight years.

Question: What type of tenant improvement package can I expect?

Poor answer: Our standard package is paint and carpet.

Better answer: The tenant improvement allowance is one facet of the lease package that depends on your space plan, square footage, rent, and so on. We typically work through those points in a proposal when we can address the whole package and have a better sense of what your company needs.

Lead the Tour

DAY-OF-TOUR PREP

On tour day, visit the space yourself. There, you can pick up junk mail that's been left, make sure the key works, turn on all the lights, and open the blinds. If you ask maintenance staff to complete these tasks, ensure that they understand your standards so the suite looks good when the prospective tenants arrive.

A LITMUS TEST

The basics—greeting people by name, a firm handshake, eye contact, warmth, and property knowledge instill confidence that a building (and landlord) is a good match. That's because, as the tour guide, you embody the landlord. Even if you do not ultimately manage the building and may not even negotiate the entire lease deal, leasing representatives serve as a proxy for the landlord. Tenants wonder if you will be a good landlord. Can they trust you? In fact, Kingsley Associates research suggests that tenants do not differentiate between an independent contractor—such as a landscaper—and an employee, such as the property manager in charge of leasing.[7] The tenants perceive *any* people working at the property as an extension of the ownership, regardless of their employment status and relationship to the landlord. As such, image and attitude become paramount for all building staff, from receptionist to engineer to property manager.

> *I once toured visitors from a large foreign engineering company. Although the session went well, the engineering firm executive wanted to negotiate with a representative who held a title equivalent to his own. My company quickly allowed me a commensurate title in order to get the deal done. The next day, the ink barely dry, I handed out a printed business card with a newfound title: Leasing Executive. (Luckily, I hadn't had a card inside the marketing materials folder.) We went on to complete the deal. Negotiators have to feel that each side is empowered to make decisions, and thus, titles can be meaningful. And other times, culture can influence negotiations. (This incident begs the story of a promotion and salary bump, but that's for another day.)*

ESTABLISH A RAPPORT WITH THE BROKER

Typically, brokers accompany prospective tenants on a tour. By showing respect, you strengthen your relationships. Shake hands with brokers and allow them to introduce their clients. Then, you might acknowledge the broker's relationship with the landlord, especially if it's been a positive one.

> *I had a college buddy who enjoyed a career as a prominent commercial office broker. When he arrived at the building and we shook hands, he would squeeze my hand in a secret handshake. It took everything I had not to burst out laughing. Joking aside, I would turn to the client and say "You have a great broker. Peter has brought us stellar tenants over the years, and we look forward to working with all of you." That way, everyone would know that we enjoyed a good working relationship. The broker knew he was valued and the tenants knew they were in good hands (no pun intended).*

DECISION MAKERS AND MOLES

When a tenant arrives to the tour, pay special attention to introductions. At this stage, you can often identify decision makers as well as discern how much influence the broker wields. In addition to the chief executive on tour, some leasing agents look for a mole, although not of the rodent variety. Shorthand for the employee that works closely with the company's principals, the mole may be an office manager or administrative assistant. More accessible than the decision maker and less burdened with negotiation

A Critical Question

Where does the prospective tenant's decision maker live? Most executives won't voluntarily choose a long commute.

responsibility, a mole can provide valuable information about the tenant's leasing process, criteria, preferences, and concerns. Good agents identify and cultivate this relationship over the course of the deal, starting with the tour.

A COMPELLING STORY

One of the basic tenets of leasing is learning about your prospect. Good landlords take a proactive approach to understanding tenant needs. Asking the prospective tenant the open-ended "tell me about your ideal office space" question before giving an overview of your property allows you to hear a tenant's priorities. This type of dialogue also provides a barometer of how happy tenants are in their current space and helps you target your leasing pitch by emphasizing pertinent information during the tour.

In particular, leasing personnel often grapple with the issue of why a tenant is considering a move. This rationale informs you of tenant priorities and allows your highest and best use of resources. For instance, expending a significant amount of time on a tenant who is merely shopping the market might allow other viable prospects to slip away to properties where they are showered with time and attention. So it's up to you to evaluate tenants in order to best allocate leasing energies.

Some agents start by assuming tenants do not want to move, unless the tenant gives a compelling reason. Why? Because the thought of moving makes even the most competent office manager reach for an entire bottle of aspirin. It's expensive, time consuming, and inconvenient. So listen closely. Do the tenants' reasons for moving make sense? If so, you have viable prospects. If not, the tenants may be exercising you to compete against their existing landlords for a better lease renewal.

> **The thought of moving makes even the most competent office manager reach for an entire bottle of aspirin. It's expensive, time consuming, and inconvenient. So listen closely. Do the reasons the tenant or broker give for relocation make sense? If so, you have viable prospects.**

Lease long enough, and you'll see the common reasons that tenants move. They include a tenant needing more or less space than an existing landlord can accommodate, a changed business that necessitates amenities such as more parking or airport proximity, a change in the tenant company's management (the decision maker wants a shorter commute), and so on. In general, the more specifics tenants offer, the greater the likelihood that they are serious about relocating the office. Most landlords loathe losing an expanding (and thus, usually profitable) tenant. So unless you know that the prospect's current building does not have any expansion space or other tenants dominate the rights to potential expansion space, the prospect may not be viable. And be wary of tenants who badmouth or have adversarial relationships with their current landlords. Is the tenant difficult to deal with? Does the tenant pay bills on time? Again, landlords don't like to see solid, rent-paying tenants leave.

Last, let your instincts be your guide. The best leasing personnel have an ability to determine congruence between what someone says and the physical cues (face, tone of voice, posture) that accompany those statements. Whether innate or learned, this facet of emotional intelligence is an important tool in assessing prospects . . . and deciding how to allocate your leasing energy.

FIVE QUESTIONS TO ASK ON THE TOUR

- ☐ Why are you leaving your existing building?
- ☐ What is your current office location?
- ☐ Where do your employees live?
- ☐ Where does the decision maker live?
- ☐ Can you describe your ideal office space?

THAT WARM AND FUZZY FEELING

When a tour is going well, you will feel a sense of engagement from the tenant and the broker, often demonstrated by eye contact, thoughtful questions, and time spent on the tour. Professionals consider a tenant who talks and provides feedback on the tour an indicator of a successful tour. When your instincts tell you all systems are go, zero in on the next step for that tenant by asking to schedule a space planning meeting and where to send the proposal to lease.

RECOVER FROM THE INEVITABLE GOOFS

The chef's equivalent of a kitchen fire at dinnertime, awkward and challenging moments will arise during tours.

While problems are guaranteed, it is the response that determines if you end up with dinner or disaster.

The following challenges are among the most typical. For example, a prospective tenant may arrive with an entourage worthy of a rock star. Outnumbered, you can be barraged with questions from ten individuals. Even the playing field by enlisting warm bodies; anyone with a pulse is fair game. Have the assistant property manager or building engineer accompany this group. Make a deft change by telling the client you are delighted to welcome a large group and say you'd like to ask for other members of the building management team to accompany the group in order to create a better tour. This shows the landlord's ability to offer service and flexibility. Introduce these members of the management team who will ultimately work with the tenant. Your coworkers can help divide and conquer as they converse with members of the group (or unlock doors or push the elevator button), and you will be free to direct the tour and focus your energies on the decision makers.

Or, prospective tenants might arrive for a tour but refuse to divulge their company's name. Relax. After all, some entity has to sign a lease. Savvy agents do not take offense, and assume there is good reason for anonymity. For instance, large or prestigious companies may be hovering on the verge of confidential business changes. Let the name go (for now). Rather, focus on information about the prospect's business. Ask defining questions such as: Will the type of employees housed in this office drive their own cars or use public transportation (i.e., sales/executives or back-office space)? Do you prefer private offices (potential traditional corporation) or an open layout (potential technology firm)? Over time, you will gain a sense of the company culture that hints at the nature of a business.

> **Talking Commission on a Tour? No**
> Sometimes, inexperienced brokers will question commission policies mid-tour; use a friendly manner to tell the broker you will call later that day to confirm brokerage issues. It's best not to sideline the tour with the broker's compensation matters.

With experience, you can craft your own positive solutions to tour challenges. In the meantime, however, think mitigation. The solution does not need to be perfect; you are just looking to improve the immediate situation. Afterward, ask effective leasing agents how they would have handled the situation. Experience and practice can turn difficult situations to your advantage, and at the very least, lend variety to your workday.

Here's how I once recovered from a tour gone awry: I had toured an insurance company seeking 5,000 square feet of office space through a suburban building south of San Francisco. Although the decision maker lived in San Francisco, she wanted accessible parking as well as some budget predictability as the city imposed a changing stream of taxes. Designed by renowned Gensler architects, the newly constructed Class A building offered a stunning glass atrium entrance with leafy green trees, easy parking access, and top-notch improvements including a fitness center and conference facility.

The tenant loved the building until she walked into the suite. Her face fell. As real estate people, we can envision the gray concrete shell of new space transformed into a lovely office. As lay people, the tenant sees a gray concrete shell. I tried to create a vision by visiting a nearby finished tenant suite, but the tenant still doubted the vacant space would look as good. Then, I finished the tour and let the company know we would love to have them as a tenant.

The next day, I asked the decision maker if she would come have lunch with me. Luckily, I got a second chance—the manager agreed. I raced to ask my contractor to hang the standard two-by-four-foot suspended light fixtures from the concrete slab above. By the next morning, the entire suite was illuminated (although it lacked an acoustical ceiling). It changed the space significantly. When the prospect revisited, she was pleased with the bright, pleasant suite. Moreover, after years of indifference from her existing landlord, she was impressed with our speed, creativity, and drive to solve a problem. We landed the company as a tenant and enjoyed many years of a solid relationship, which included two office expansions over the next seven years.

After the Tour

SOME SELF-REFLECTION

After the tour, take a few moments to reflect on what went well (and what didn't). It's a great practice to jot down some notes while the memories are fresh, whether it's information about the decision maker or a specific request about the space. To grow into a better agent, assess every tour.

And if asked, most brokers will also evaluate the tour, giving you valuable insight on strengths (and weaknesses) of your presentation along with tenant perceptions. Lower your defenses and listen—you may be surprised how others respond to your high level of conscientious service.

THANKS AND CONTINUE THE CONVERSATION

Conventional protocol advises thanking others within twenty-four hours—via email, text, telephone, or note. As a bonus, a telephone call, with its ability for dialogue and nuance, allows us to gauge tenant interest in the space. Also, consider writing or emailing a note of thanks for their time to both the broker and tenant. Be sure to direct emails to both the brokers and tenants so you do not cause undue concern for the brokers that they will not be recognized (in the event of a commission). Regardless of a consummated lease, these gracious actions build relationships that help you in the long run . . . and make life a little more civil.

In addition to a polite thank you, some leasing personnel utilize a tour to initiate ongoing contact with the prospective tenant and broker. As an example, following up with a floor plan, the answer to a question, or simply additional information extends your relationships by creating opportunities for potential dialogue. And if, during the tour, you promise to send a floor plan or get back to the broker or tenant with information, do it immediately. As author Wallace Stegner's character Larry Lang from the novel *Crossing to Safety* asks, "Can I think of anyone in my whole life whom I have liked without his first showing signs of liking me?"[8] All prospects want to know that a landlord wants them, because attentive landlords value and treat their tenants well.

As author Wallace Stegner's character Larry Lang from the novel *Crossing to Safety* asks, "Can I think of anyone in my whole life whom I have liked without his first showing signs of liking me?"[9] All prospects want to know that a landlord wants them, because attentive landlords value and treat their tenants well.

After the tour, contact the tenant's broker (or the tenant, if not represented) on a weekly basis, noting the prospect's leasing status. As part of your follow-up, prospective tenants may want to revisit the space or bring others from the company. This extremely positive sign shows that the tenants envision themselves in the space, and soon, you may be asked to submit a proposal for lease. Most tenants will progress to the proposal stage or move on to another building within a month. Sometimes, prospective tenants will return if negotiations at another building go awry, so act politely and professionally if a tenant initially passes on your property. And ask the broker what made the other property work better initially so that you might close the gap on any competitive differences.

CHAPTER 6

Create a Space Plan

"It's not just what it looks like and feels like. Design is how it works."[1]
—*Steve Jobs, co-founder, Apple Inc.*

GOAL: CREATE A PRACTICAL, APPEALING SPACE PLAN FOR A TENANT WITHIN BUDGET SO THE LANDLORD CAN ESTIMATE CONSTRUCTION COSTS AND STRUCTURE A LEASE DEAL THAT PENCILS

Note: *architect* and *space planner* are used as interchangeable terms in this chapter.

With pencil poised over tracing paper, an architect sketches plans for a new office. A cornice here, a spotlight there. Five minutes and four exposed brick walls later, the space planning meeting has careened wildly out of control.

The property manager silently rehearses ways to tell the prospective tenant it cannot afford this Taj Mahal of an office. This all-too-common dilemma can arise because of miscommunication between the leasing representative and the architect, poor timing, or unrealistic expectations on the tenant's part. Space planning, the initial layout sketch of a prospective suite, informs the level of tenant improvements, which then influence the financial package of the entire lease deal. You, the leasing representative, must guide the process so as to arrive at a space plan that fits both the tenant's vision and the landlord's wallet.

So how do you work with a prospective tenant and architect to design a suitable space and, in doing so, move toward a signed lease deal? Specific office layouts are a result of each tenant's values, priorities, work style, and, yes, budget. And while the process resembles a loose recipe more than a precise formula, cutting a bit of this and emphasizing some of that, great space plans do result from the following general practices.

Time It Right

In large part, space plans succeed because of appropriate timing. Early in the leasing process, the landlord and tenant haven't agreed on economic terms yet, including the tenant improvement budget. As such, space planning without economic parameters becomes nearly impossible. But if space planning is deferred too long, tenants may latch on to a competing building where they can visualize themselves and have become economically and emotionally invested in the space.

As an additional layer of complexity, market conditions influence space plan timing, as landlords typically bear space planning expenses. In tight markets with few vacancies, landlords may require a signed letter of (lease) intent prior to space planning. In soft markets, landlords may commit space planning resources once they evaluate a tenant as a viable prospect and not one simply shopping the market to use in renewal negotiations with its existing building. Wise landlords gauge the local market before investing space planning dollars, to get the most bang for their architectural buck.

EVALUATE YOUR PROSPECT

To proceed with your own space planning, evaluate the prospect within the context of the local market. First, consider the prospective company's viability as a tenant. Because landlords typically foot the bill for space planning expenses, tenants can exert pressure to complete a space plan simply because it's all upside for them (i.e., the chance to plan future offices) with little downside. The planning process adds value for tenants whether or not they sign a lease at a particular building. As such, the landlord needs to decide if the tenant is a real prospect. Otherwise, you squander dollars creating plans for companies that fail to sign leases and, in a worst-case scenario, help your competitor's building by designing offices for its tenant on your dime.

Another important consideration is your property's electrical capacity relative to the prospective tenant's needs. In recent years, population density and the prevalence of electronics place demands on building infrastructures (especially true for older properties). Understanding your properties' capabilities relative to tenant demand will become crucial to proceeding with any proposed deal.

Should You Open Your Space-Planning Purse?

- Do the tenant's credit and financial statements appear strong?
- Is your building the tenant's first or second choice?
- How generous are your competitors in terms of space planning services?

Review the Financials

Although a prospective tenant's financial strength should ideally be assessed prior to space planning, many landlords proceed with space planning based on a somewhat loose understanding of financial strength and company integrity. Space planning expenses are generally considered a necessary marketing expense. The whole process is a little chicken and egg; without a bona fide prospect you do not do a space plan, but without the space plan you may not be able to convert a prospect into a tenant. At the end of the day, space planning remains a calculated risk and necessary marketing expense.

Evaluate the Prospect's Interest in the Space

Does your prospective tenant have a vision? Oftentimes, you can gauge a tenant's interest by the forethought the tenant demonstrates. When prospective tenants speak as if they already occupy the space and have specific requests, they are envisioning themselves as occupants. Conversely,

---

Just a Paint Swatch, Please

Sometimes, space plans prove unnecessary. If the suite can suffice with cosmetic changes such as paint and carpet, the tenant chooses from building standards or engages an interior designer for minimal time and cost. *As is* (or almost as is) spaces can work for tenants on a tight budget or with brief lease terms, in an effort to reduce costs and keep rent low.

---

when tenants cannot articulate their needs and make no specific references to the suite, the space plan might be just an exercise (on your dime).

Assess Within the Context of the Market

Sometimes, circumstances—either a tough leasing market or a red-hot prospect—necessitate a space plan before a landlord can qualify a tenant's financials. One solution to this dilemma is for the tenant to indemnify the landlord for the cost of the space plan until the tenant provides solid financials. (Refer to appendix B for an indemnification letter when proposing such an arrangement to the tenant.) Once the landlord reviews the financials and decides that the tenant prospect would have qualified for space planning, the indemnification disappears. Another, even better, solution is for the tenants to pay for the architect and have the landlord reimburse them once the financials have been reviewed and approved.

> Sometimes, circumstances—like a red-hot prospect who's in a rush—necessitate a space plan before a landlord can qualify a tenant's financials. One solution to this dilemma is for the tenant to indemnify the landlord for the cost of the space plan until the tenant provides solid financials.

As a note of caution, while indemnification letters allow the parties to leapfrog the natural deal progression, they can lessen pressure on both parties to deliver promised items. If a tenant pays for its own space planning because of the chore of collating financial information, both the landlord and tenant can be tempted to proceed full steam ahead. Later, should the tenant reveal its weak credit, choosing not to consummate the lease becomes more difficult as both parties have invested time and resources. So use space planning indemnification letters judiciously, opting instead to complete the crucial credit check process in most cases (more on that later).

I once showed space to a Fortune 500 tenant whose decision maker wanted the deal–the terms and space plan–tied up in one neat package. He planned to review the deal in the airport lounge, between flights. The office manager knew that without an office layout scheme, the decision maker's attention would shift to other concerns or another building. Because of the company's sterling reputation and the office manager's confidence that the decision maker would like the suite, I made an exception. Prior to reviewing the formal tenant financials, I agreed to bear the immediate expense for a space plan. The office manager and architect developed a space plan that afternoon. Before the airplane's wheels lifted, the executive approved the deal and we moved on to the formal proposal stage.

Understand Space Planning Expenses

Commercial space planning costs can account for a quarter to nearly one-third of the total architectural expenses, which include full-blown construction documents. According to Archinect, an online discussion forum for architects, space planning costs are approximately $0.35 per square foot with complete architectural drawings hovering around $1.25 to $1.50 per square foot. So your typical 5,000 square-foot tenant will cost $1,750 in architectural fees for space planning alone, enough to toggle the marketing needle. Even with the reduced costs of an in-house planner or office planning software, space planning still amounts to money and time.

While the tenant may not feel the pinch of the space planning expense initially, such costs may become part of the eventual lease terms. In order to recoup funds, space planning costs may be amortized at current interest rates over the lease term into the tenant's rent.

A Fat Wallet

The American Institute of Architects (www. aia.org) provides cost information on space planning and construction documentation, which vary by market.

COMMUNICATE THE BUDGET TO THE ARCHITECT

The interconnected nature of space planning and tenant improvements, and thus rent, makes understanding the budget critical. While it's not the architect's job to negotiate rental rates, common sense tells you that it's prudent to have the architect understand the deal parameters. Further, if a tenant plans to contribute tenant improvement dollars for the space, the architect should confer with the tenant at intervals to make the design fit the tenant's desires and pocketbook. Otherwise, the tenant won't get that living green wall that's undeliverable on a bare-bones budget.

> *I know a wry developer who says he stays within "shin-kicking distance" of his architect. The quip underscores the importance of a landlord's communication with the architect in order to design a space the parties can afford. It's hard to recover from dashed expectations when the tenant learns the designed space is way over budget. In fact, it may be enough to drive them from the building. After all, if the landlord and architect don't communicate well enough to create a workable space plan, what does that say about the landlord's professionalism?*

Run an Effective Space Planning Meeting

The space planning meeting is where the tenant, architect or designer, and landlord's representative gather to design the tenant space. By organizing the various aspects of the space planning meeting, you allow the lease process to proceed. Here's how:

STAY AT THE HUB

The most effective leasing agents act as sane traffic controllers at the hub of a deal, directing the process. Creating space plans provides the landlord with an understanding of the tenant's business, preferences, likes and dislikes, and office culture. Further, good landlords recognize space planning as an absolutely critical bonding time in the lease process. Controlling? You bet. Resist the temptation to delegate the process to the architect or contractor. In this role, you host all meetings; approve all correspondence, estimates, and plans before they are sent to the tenant; and oversee the completion of all work. Moreover, your oversight and attention to detail indicate a high level of service to your prospective tenants as they choose a landlord.

THE RIGHT GUEST LIST

From the building owner's side, invite the landlord's leasing representative and the architect to the initial space planning meeting. From the tenant's side, the decision-making executive in charge of the office, along with the office manager, should attend. Sometimes the tenant delegates the task internally to an employee who doesn't have decision-making power, or worse, to a large committee. Either of these scenarios is a recipe for disaster. In the first instance, individuals without enough clout can fail to articulate space needs, oftentimes because of political considerations or long-term business goals they might not understand. In the second scenario, large groups can require a lot of work to reach consensus.

As the fearless leasing leader, your task is to ensure that you invite meeting attendees who have the decision-making authority to arrive at a viable space plan. Ask

Red Flag Warning
Your antenna should perk up if the tenant's decision maker declines your invitation to the space planning meeting, as it may signal a disinterest in the potential suite (and in doing a deal at your property).

yourself (and the tenant) where the buck stops, and then extend invitations to those people. If the executive in charge declines to attend, ask if the individual that will attend has decision-making authority. Explain that the space planning budget allows for an initial plan with only minor revision so the tenant recognizes the significance of creating a quality plan at the first meeting. Finally, if the prospective tenant has an in-house planner or facility person (often toting a company standard layout), all is well because the tenant's internal team will have experience mapping out the office configuration.

ADDING ENGINEERING OR MECHANICAL EXPERTS

Sometimes a tenant expresses concern over a mechanical or technical aspect of the building. In those situations, invite your building engineers (or subcontractors) if they articulate technical issues well. If engineers do attend the meeting, they usually depart after addressing any building-systems discussions and do not stay for the remainder of the space planning meeting. This added level of service speaks to the landlord's willingness to hire experts to handle tenant concerns.

A Building's Integrity

Whether the landlord engages a general contractor or allows tenants to provide their own, most landlords specify the subcontractors that can affect building systems: approved plumbers, electricians, HVAC, and roofing contractors. Also, those landlords who do permit outside contractors insist on a review-and-approval procedure for plans and construction.

ADVANCE PREPARATION

You—and possibly the space planner—should visit the tenant's existing office in advance of the meeting, noting the differences between the existing space and the prospective suite. This visit may help ascertain any special space needs the tenant has overlooked. Also, visiting a tenant's existing space gives you a deeper look into that world. The more you learn about your clients, the more you can service and negotiate with them, both for architectural purposes and other lease issues. Is the company bursting out of the space? Then you should have a motivated prospect, ready to reach agreement in good time. Is the parking lot packed with cars? If so, your building with ample parking will look attractive and you can emphasize the easy access. Your observations will help you capitalize on the advantages your property offers, both during the initial space planning meeting and beyond.

Our finish board that displays building-standard paint colors, carpet samples, and baseboard and countertop materials is the envy of Vanna White. It simplifies all the finish choices for the tenant. Oftentimes, lease decision makers will defer to the office manager's (or someone else's) selection of such finishes, engaging them in the leasing process. After all, most people appreciate having a say in their office environment.

CHECKLIST: THE RIGHT MATERIALS ON HAND

☐ As-built blueprints (or at a minimum, a floor plan)

☐ Building-standard finish boards (including paint colors)

☐ Building-standard carpet choices

☐ Building-standard laminate and/or stone samples

☐ Tracing paper

☐ Pens and pencils

☐ Architect's (scaled) ruler

☐ Tape measure

☐ Keys to unlock the vacant suite, for an impromptu visit

☐ Any computer-aided design (CAD) tools, if appropriate

☐ Computer charging cords

☐ Virtual reality tools/technology, if used

Note: while CAD sketch tools have become prominent in the architectural and construction fields, tracing paper and pencils have their brainstorming advantages.

THE MEETING KICKOFF

At the start of the meeting, introduce the architect and explain the space planning process to the prospective tenant, who may be inexperienced in office design. Tell the tenant that the architect will ask a series of programming questions to ascertain the tenant's most critical needs, such as "Do you need a conference room, and if so, for how many?" and "Do you prefer an open or closed office plan?" Then, the architect prepares a preliminary sketch of a potential office with the tenant's input. By the close of the meeting, the goal is to reach a workable design that the tenant can take home and the landlord can send out for construction estimates.

SPEAKING THE LANGUAGE

Architects speak a strange geometric language of lines, dots, triangles, and circles. In order to become fluent, you need to translate these symbols into windows, walls, and doors. Most space plans and construction documents contain a *legend*, a guide to the symbol shorthand, typically printed in the lower corner of a plan. For example, a wall that is to be demolished will be indicated with dashed lines, while a newly constructed wall (or partition, as it's called) will be shown with a solid line. As you learn to decipher the various symbols—probably twenty or so of the most common—plans will become much easier and quicker to read.

Further, plans are *scaled* so that a particular measurement (often one-quarter inch) equates to one linear foot. Again, refer to the plan's legend to understand its orientation and scale. While space plans are abbreviated, single-page drawings of an office, they will eventually be translated into detailed, multipage construction documents.

I use my understanding of architectural symbols to communicate in code. For instance, when I ask my architect if a sidelight might work as well as glass block in an office, I'm telling him to suggest a less costly alternative without expressly saying such in front of the tenant. Of course, using this language assumes you know your unit prices so that you realize glass block costs significantly more than a side-lit piece of glass. Learning the symbols and their costs allows me proficiency in design.

DO YOU SPEAK ARCHITECTESE?

- ☐ NIC: not included in contract
- ☐ Plan view: a bird's-eye view, the perspective from looking down at a space
- ☐ Elevation view: a frontal view, as if you are standing on the ground looking at the space in front of you
- ☐ CDs: construction documents
- ☐ Duplex: an electrical outlet with two receptacles
- ☐ Fourplex: an electrical outlet with four receptacles
- ☐ Partition: a wall, usually stopping at the ceiling level
- ☐ Slab to slab: a (fire-rated) wall, built from the floor to the underside of the next floor
- ☐ CAD: computer-aided design (three-dimensional drawings)
- ☐ Scale: the proportional size of the drawing to the actual space (usually one-quarter or one-eighth inch equals one foot)

COMPUTER-AIDED DESIGN

Technology allows easy display of existing floor plans and suite improvements; however, many architects use a hybrid approach to the space planning stage. While architects access electronic layouts, they may also use traditional pencil and tracing paper in this brainstorming process. Then, after a satisfactory space plan is reached, the architect will convert the approved layouts to an electronic form. On the other hand, some architects work exclusively with computer-aided design. It depends on the market, the extent of planning needed, and, to some degree, the architect's preference. Increasingly, virtual reality is used to illustrate a space, a boon for clients who lack three-dimensional visualization skills. While architects, contractors, and landlords are adopting this technology, it has yet to completely infiltrate the market. In the meantime, keep your tracing paper and printed floor plan.

On the tenant side, more sophisticated (usually large) tenants administer space via electronic tools. For instance, software allows firms to manage every seat in the office. Click on any color-coded department and you'll see the lease terms associated with the group, along with details like telephone privileges, internet/intranet access, furniture standards, and so on. The client can circle a department and then "drop it" onto another floor, in a hypothetical move scenario. The program will show the facility manager a new configuration and create a detailed move to-do list. From a space planning perspective, count your lucky stars if you have tenants this savvy, because they have a firm handle on their real estate wants, needs, and wallet.

Lead Time

The time required for producing space plans varies based on square footage and design complexity. In general, for small suites (1,500 square feet or under), the tenant should be able to leave the meeting with a preliminary space plan in hand. For larger suites, aim for a turnaround of two to five days.

Know Design Trends: Hotel, Motel, Holiday Inn?

Staying abreast of office design trends allows you to give your building relevance in the marketplace as you compete for prospective tenants. As fickle as fashion, tenant improvements oscillate between modernist, with its exposed ducts, and traditional, where the corner office reigns supreme. Existing building architecture, too, can influence design. But more frequently, it's company culture and cost that drive the office layouts du jour.

LET'S GET PHYSICAL

Functional physical spaces are critical to business endeavors. Although technology surrounds us, it has not eliminated the need for physical space. Virtual reality? Yes. Virtual everything? Well, not quite. Ironically, technology companies seem to value physical workspaces even more than the average bear. For example, consider the organic restaurants, concierge services, and sand volleyball courts that dot Silicon Valley's corporate campuses. In addition to reducing the need to leave work for personal errands, the

Whiteboards All Around

From offices where employees name the conference rooms, indulging their travel fantasies—Kilimanjaro, Sedona, Bangkok— to offices with interior columns wrapped in whiteboard material, today's companies seek employee input on office space.

interaction driven by physical proximity lies at the heart of many companies' creativity and, thus, culture and success.

COLLABORATION AND COLLISION

Open plans tout collaboration and a lack of hierarchy, where the company CEO works alongside other employees. Ring the office with exposed brick and toss in room for a Ping-Pong table or a slide that connects floors and there you have it: possibly more playground than office, a space that infuses fun into the long hours at work. Alright, while a slide is an extreme example, these tenant improvements underscore the value companies place on making the office experience enjoyable and connecting employees.

In a recent trend, firms are forging new design by creating spaces for workers to encounter others, independent of their role within the firm. The notion behind the design is that true innovation results from "chance encounters and unplanned interactions between knowledge workers, both inside and outside the organization,"[2] according to the sociometric data gathered in a study published by the *Harvard Business Review*. In a similar show of promoting chance meetings, Google has placed coffee and food bars throughout its offices, with employees rarely more than 200 feet from artisan treats. Food, like art or dogs, is a social object, meaning it encourages human interaction. Yesterday's water cooler has become today's espresso bar, but it serves the same purpose: to connect people. How does this translate to tenant improvements? It means more open spaces and corridors for people to meet, central seating areas, food, drinks, a view, outdoor meeting areas, artwork, and so on. Many companies value creativity and collaboration, and they seek to work in spaces that mirror and encourage these attributes through proximity.

> **Yesterday's water cooler has become today's espresso bar, but it serves the same purpose: to connect people.**

At the other end of the office design spectrum lie private offices, with regulated sizes marching alongside each other up to the corner office, a literal ladder of corporate hierarchy. Businesses such as family law firms and wealth managers require closed doors for confidentiality, making private offices a must. In addition, Gloria Mark, a professor at the University of California, Irvine, makes a further case for privacy. Although Professor Mark's research shows that employee interruptions led to faster work (as the employees compensated for lost time), "people in the interrupted conditions experienced a higher workload, more stress, higher frustration, more time pressure, and effort."[3] While Mark delves into the distinctions between good interruptions and unproductive interruptions, the bottom line is that some workers require spaces free from the hurly-burly of disruption.

While companies decide how office form will follow function, even traditional companies are modifying their wood-paneled, corner-office configurations. In a survey of major US law firms, the *Wall Street Journal* reported that firms were "shrinking private offices, swapping out walls for glass, and installing high-tech meeting rooms in dead space once occupied by law libraries and filing cabinets."[4] In an effort to lower costs and boost productivity, offices now feature areas for attorneys to collaborate, along with smaller private office spaces.

Charles Darwin had nothing on the real estate industry: change or die. Recently, the managing partner of a national brokerage company illustrated a changed way of working that impacts office space. The partner told me he'd paid two undergrad students for a week during winter break, giving each his own cubicle, landline, and computer. Then, he tasked them with scrubbing a huge contact list of companies. Within hours, the two hulking young men were huddled in one cubicle. Using their cell phones, a laptop, and websites "you've never heard of," they secured contact names, contact information, addresses, and personal information. The partner referenced the notion of benching, in which employees pull up chairs to a long table. Impressed by the interns' results, the managing partner said his next hires were going to be hungry young employees who knew the true meaning of collaboration . . . not to mention they wouldn't need a lot of office space.[5]

ECONOMICS OF DESIGN

Other factors, such as the state of the market, also influence design. During economic downturns, space planning tends toward more generic spaces to allow for company flexibility. It's somewhat of an art, because even small changes in size can dramatically influence a space's practicality. For example, standard offices may measure ten by twelve feet while a larger thirteen-by-fifteen-foot office allows for additional conferencing. Build a twelve-by-fifteen-foot office, though, and you have neither fish nor fowl; it has more space than needed for a desk, credenza, and side chair but does not accommodate typical conference room furniture. When salvaging traditional spaces, architects often retain the existing perimeter offices

Hoteling

Companies plan for the nomadic employee (and maximize square footage) by providing a desk, plug-and-play capability, modular furniture, and lockers for personal belongings.

even when creating open interior spaces because it minimizes construction costs and allows for some privacy. Construction in the corners is particularly costly because of separately zoned HVAC and lighting, and added demolition expenses.

GREEN SPACE

Excellent space planning demands a green consciousness in today's real estate industry. Oftentimes, the most expedient way to green a space is to reuse existing tenant improvements that have value. Consider the labor and materials involving in making an office several feet larger—simply moving a wall involves demolition, lighting, fire suppression, ceiling tile, HVAC, drywall, insulation, electrical, carpet, baseboard, and paint subcontractors. Whew. Unless there is true value gained by moving walls, it is much greener to work within existing parameters. Recycled elements can still be burnished so they have contemporary appeal. For instance, brick walls can be treated so that their weathered components lend an industrial, contemporary vibe to offices.

WAYS TO GREEN A SPACE

☐ Minimize window-line offices to allow in more natural light.

☐ Use atriums and skylights.

☐ Place windows strategically for day lighting and lower cooling costs (sometimes even a code requirement).

☐ Use carpet made from recycled materials and solvent alternatives.

☐ Install recycled-denim wall insulation.

☐ Minimize code compliance expenses with an analysis of existing configurations.

☐ Use the finish display board (and brochures and websites) to communicate your sustainable commitment by identifying nontoxic or environmentally friendly paint or natural fibers.

Deliver the Space Plan

After a productive planning meeting, the next step is to present the space plan to the tenant. Tenants often complete preliminary space plans with one or two competing buildings prior to making a final lease decision, so delivering a quality space plan—especially if the planning process went smoothly—can entice a tenant to a building, quantify construction costs, and cement a lease deal.

IMPROVING READABILITY

Most importantly, present the plan in an easily readable format. The plan should display only relevant details that help the tenant envision the space, such as labeled rooms (e.g., office, kitchen, etc.) and a furniture layout. Refrain from overloading your prospect with too much clutter; after all, the tenant is making a business decision, not earning an engineering degree. Note: the plan going to the contractor might contain more technical, detailed information for estimating purposes, but there's little need for tenants to receive this copy, which might overwhelm them. Additionally, some landlords create a less politically charged experience by providing the tenant with two drawings. The first identifies the various offices with specific employee names while the second plan indicates office space only. Office moves can spawn a host of political issues that managers massage with various office layouts. With a clean plan devoid of individual names, the tenant can plot employee locations and circulate the plan without generating a rash of premature discussions regarding office assignments. Ask your tenants if they would prefer these two types of drawings—they may appreciate your consideration.

Last, indicate the rentable square footage but omit the usable square footage. Listing both numbers prompts tenants to focus on the amount of space for which they pay rent but do not use. The delta between usable and rentable square footage is known as the *common area load factor* and varies from building to building depending on its common spaces: lobby, corridors, and so on. The load factor is better left as a business discussion rather than a space plan point.

Keep the momentum of a tenant's excitement with a new office space by delivering a space plan quickly, in person if possible. While it's expedient to email the plan, it's easy to lose an email attachment. Further, your face-to-face review speaks to your level of service, a hallmark of superb landlords. Remember, at this stage, it's all about building rapport, rapport, rapport. The personal delivery also ensures the plan's safe arrival, making it less likely that a tenant shopping the market will simply forward an electronic copy of the space plan to competing buildings. (A titled building name, address, and a "read only" designation also dissuade users from copying plans.) Remember, it's courting time. Woo them with a personalized note, letting the tenants know you look forward to welcoming them to the building.

After our space planning meeting, I realized my prospective tenant had a tough time visualizing the discussed space. Planning works especially well for those who have great spatial skills, or just a good imagination. While some architects use CAD drawings or can create a three-dimensional plan, these aren't always cost-effective or available options. In order to feel comfortable, the prospective tenant needed to see the space in his mind's eye. So I asked the architect to add some extras to customize the office. She sketched a large leafy plant in the corner of the reception room, drew a sofa, guest chairs and furniture, indicated glass with arrows, and finally, labeled the door with the company name along with the principals' first names indicated on each private office. She even added some colored pencil: green, gray, and blue. Bingo, an easy-to-read plan personalized for the tenant. A picture truly can be worth a thousand words.

REVIEWING IN PERSON

Arrange a brief in-person meeting with the tenant at the same time that you deliver the space plan.

To kick off the review, identify the path of travel as if you are walking through the space (assuming you are working from a two-dimensional plan. If it's a three-dimensional CAD drawing, you'll play tour guide, albeit less actively). Note the architect's scale of the drawing to actual linear foot, and then point out the electrical outlet locations, conference areas, kitchen, storage spaces, offices, and so on. This type of review allows the tenant to give immediate feedback. Should the tenant have any minor changes or discover errors, you can relay these to the architect for prompt revision.

REVISING THE SPACE PLAN

Most landlords plan on minor revisions to the space plan as a result of the review. Typically, you can communicate such changes to the architect, who then prepares another version of the space plan for the tenant's approval. Occasionally, tenants will want major revisions—perhaps prompted by a changed company strategy or an executive's direction—and in that case, leasing professionals usually assess the extent of the changes, the expense to modify the plans, and the likelihood of this particular tenant signing a lease. It's all fair game for more consideration and, possibly, negotiation.

Obtain Construction Cost Estimates

Once approved by the tenant, the space plan goes to the building contractor for pricing. Again, turnaround time is critical, and you should receive a written, detailed line-by-line estimate in two to five days. Moreover, if you have done your space planning well, you should have had a ballpark idea of costs prior to receiving the contractor's estimate. Should there be a significant differential between

Cost Data

You can obtain national cost data books for construction costs from CMD (www. cmdgroup.com), but it's best to have your local contractor help you understand unit costs, as they vary widely according to geography.

your expectations and the contractor's estimate, revisit each expense item line by line with the contractor to truly understand the estimated expenses. Remember that general contractor fees and unforeseen field conditions will absorb some dollars, so leave some budget contingency, with 3–5 percent being an appropriate margin. That way, field issues that will inevitably arise during construction won't send you screaming to the bank.

TURNKEY VERSUS TENANT IMPROVEMENT ALLOWANCE

Landlords typically arrange for construction via one of two methods: turnkey or tenant improvement allowance.

Click. Turnkey is just that; the tenants open the door to their fully constructed suite. Landlords that offer turnkey improvements, based on a plan acceptable to both the tenant and landlord, wrap the costs of such planning and construction into the lease deal. While turnkey deals are likely less of an initial headache for tenants, the tenants do lose some control as they don't review and approve each line item. Should a landlord shave some expenses during the course of construction, the landlord—rather than tenant—benefits from the savings.

Some argue that landlords might take shortcuts in turnkey construction, leaving the tenant with lower quality suite improvements. Because tenant improvements, however, are nearly all *real property* (that is, permanently affixed to the property), the landlord owns them. It doesn't make a lot of sense for a quality, long-term landlord to hurt the value of the property by installing subpar improvements. (Of course, if the landlord is unscrupulous, that's another issue, and the improvements are only the start of the tenant's potential problems.)

Conversely, if unanticipated field conditions arise in a turnkey scenario, the landlord is stuck with those expenses. Generally speaking, turnkey allowances benefit smaller tenants, whose improvements might be less complicated and who hold less negotiating leverage (and usually less construction experience) than large tenants.

Tenant improvement (TI) allowances, on the other hand, specify an amount to be spent on planning and construction on a square-foot basis. These allowances detail construction costs line by line. In tenant improvement scenarios, an accurately priced construction estimate becomes critical because lease negotiations are predicated on this anticipated cost of construction. Tenant improvement allowances require more administration and accounting time because of the tenant's continued involvement in the construction administration process.

KNOW YOUR CONSTRUCTION UNIT COSTS

Good leasing representatives have a basic knowledge of common construction costs. Educate yourself by asking your contractor to give a line item price for each of the items below (including the contractor markup). That way, you'll understand the implications of design on cost during the space planning process.

- ☐ Electrical duplex and fourplex
- ☐ One 8 foot x 10 foot partitioned office
- ☐ A sidelight window
- ☐ A sink and dishwasher (including plumbing costs)
- ☐ Paint and carpet in the building standard

APPROVE THE SPACE PLAN FOR CONSTRUCTION DOCUMENTS

Once you receive the cost estimate from the contractor and have reviewed it yourself, you'll know if you can build the suite within the deal parameters. If not, this is a good time to make any revisions to the space plan. Depending on the level of revision, the price will either stand or have to be re-estimated.

Upon approval of both the space plan and construction arrangement, landlords typically require the tenant's initials or signature: a signature block of approval should be stamped on the drawing for the tenant's initials. You can order an old-fashioned rubber stamp or print out an area on the plan that reads something like this: "Reviewed and Approved for Preparation of Construction Documents" or "Reviewed and Approved for Construction," with spaces for the date and the tenant's signature.

The signed space plan usually gets attached as an exhibit to the lease for signature. When the lease is signed, the plans are then converted into multipage formal construction documents. Complete construction documents (known as CDs) are multipage plans with separate sheets for the major subtrades (which include electrical, plumbing,

HVAC, celling plan, finishes, etc.) and are used as working construction documents for the site.

CHAPTER 7

Analyze Financials

"The net present value of vacant space is zero."[1]
—*Bill Wilson, real estate developer, William Wilson & Associates*

GOAL: UNDERSTAND FUNDAMENTAL
MATHEMATICAL CONCEPTS TO BETTER
ASSESS FINANCIAL STATEMENTS AND
TENANT CREDITWORTHINESS

Landlords need to make sure their proposed tenants have the financial wherewithal to fulfill their lease commitments. So in order to evaluate prospective tenants, landlords (and their representatives, including you) request financial reports and conduct credit checks. And while you will likely have help from your accountant and financial analysts, it's beneficial to learn about financial statements, particularly when it comes to structuring lease terms. Real

> **Real Estate Book Club**
> It's no beach read, but it is an excellent primer for math principles and their practical application to real estate: *Real Estate Math Demystified* by Steven P. Mooney.

estate requires the use of basic financial concepts such as the time value of money, net present value, future value, amortization, and capitalization rates. And once financials are assessed, real estate professionals employ various techniques for mitigating leasing risks.

Review Fundamental Financial Concepts

THE TIME VALUE OF MONEY

In business terms, time is valuable because of its opportunity cost; that is, if money isn't tied up in one venture it could be making money in another. The major premise for the time value of money is that the sooner you have money, the more it's worth (because of the opportunity to earn interest or invest it). The most conservative estimate of time value is a low-interest, insured investment with a guaranteed return, while the upper end of returns is anyone's guess. As such, the value of money (in real estate lease deals) is often compared against a conservative investment alternative, such as the interest rate on a five-year certificate of deposit. At any given point in the lease term, the principal balance is equal to the present value (term discussed below) of the remaining payments.

The time value of money applies to the rent negotiated today, as well as to your expenditures intended to entice a tenant to your property. When this concept is applied to any outlay of money—tenant improvements, commission or space planning dollars—the importance of time and outlay becomes clear.

NET PRESENT VALUE

Another central financial concept is net present value, the discounted value (at a certain point in time) of a stream of future cash flows based on an expected rate of return (interest). This concept is closely tied to the time value of money—which requires that a rate of return be assigned to capital invested over time because a dollar today is worth more than a dollar tomorrow due to its ability to generate interest. The process known as *discounting* brings money back over time using such a discount rate.

These concepts pertain to everyday leasing life in many ways. For instance, should a tenant decide it wants to terminate its lease at a certain point in time prior to the lease term expiration, you need to know the unamortized portion of leasing costs, such as tenant improvements, brokerage commissions, and future rent payments, in order to calculate an appropriate termination fee. That lease termination fee is the net present value, the amount the lease obligation is worth in today's dollars, taking into account all the future rent discounted back to the termination date.

FUTURE VALUE

The future value of money is the value that an amount of money today—the present value—will grow into at some future date, again, assuming a conservative return rate.

AMORTIZATION

Amortization refers to periodic payments, usually of equal amounts, which include repayment of the principal and the payment of interest on the declining principal balance of a loan. You charge interest for the privilege of borrowing funds, because, had you not made this loan (in the form of tenant improvements, etc.), you could have earned interest on your money elsewhere. Periodic payments are typically a fixed monthly amount with the principal and interest ratio of any individual payment varying throughout the term of the loan. The variables that affect the principal and interest portion of each loan payment are the interest rate, amortization term (length of time), periodic payment (how often a loan payment will be made), and principal amount. Three of these four variables must be known before the fourth can be determined. An example might be a tenant who wants an increase in its tenant improvement allowance. Most landlords amortize this additional allowance on top of the rent—it's a loan, with the landlord acting as the banker. Using an amortization calculation, you can help tenants understand the direct impact tenant improvements (or any other financial concessions) make on their rental rates.

CAPITALIZATION RATES

Long the standard valuation tool for the real estate industry, a capitalization (or cap) rate is a mathematical formula, expressed as a percentage. Cap rates are calculated by dividing the net operating income (NOI)—the income minus expenses—of a property by its purchase price. Logically, the rental derived as a result of leases plays into

> **Cocktail Conversation? No. Financial Literacy? Yes. Know These Facts:**
>
> - Interest on a one-year certificate of deposit (CD) and five-year CD
> - CPI (consumer price index) this year
> - Current Dow Jones Industrial Average; is the market trending up or down?
> - Current Nasdaq Composite; is the market trending up or down?
> - Current Federal Reserve interest rate

cap rates because of its impact on the net operating income of a property along with other revenue and expenses.

Cap rates and interest rates have a correlation, but the relationship is complex, and the rates aren't completely in sync with each other. It seems intuitive that interest rates and cap rates are related because the real estate's dependence on the cost of debt is a significant factor in ownership, which affects debt service expenses and consequently, the net operating income.

Use Tools

SOFTWARE

Many lease professionals use software to model lease deals and provide analysis. In some real estate companies, dedicated financial analysts complete the data entry and interpretation, while in others, the leasing professionals enter figures into formatted spreadsheet programs created to show the economic attributes of a proposed deal. Still others dispense with formal analysis, as they know what deals will pencil for their particular markets. Regardless of the method and tools, underlying financial concepts apply to every leasing deal.

FINANCIAL CALCULATORS

Run, don't walk, to the nearest office supply store (or to your computer) to purchase a financial calculator, an absolute must for real estate professionals. Popular models include the Texas Instruments BA II Plus, Hewlett Packard 12c, and other iterations such as Hewlett Packard's 10bII. While the HP 12c is an older calculator, many real estate professionals like it for its compactness. Once users become accustomed to the Polish notation (i.e., reverse entry), and the functions of a dollar, the financial calculator becomes

Dry Toast

The owner manuals that accompany financial calculators explain, in dry detail, all the functions. Many of the helpful instructions refer to leasing scenarios, such as "present value of a lease with advance payments" and "calculating a lease payment." For more training, professional organizations, such as the Institute of Real Estate Management (www.irem.org) or the Building Owners and Managers Association (www.boma.org), offer courses utilizing these calculators.

indispensable. For more assistance, online financial calculator apps are also available.

While most lease analysis comes courtesy of robust software programs, the financial calculator is great for its flexibility. Small and portable, it's easy to run some proposed tenant improvement numbers and understand that impact on rent. And while larger computer programs provide more detailed overviews and analysis, there are many aspects of the proposal and lease negotiation stages where you need quick feedback.

Applying Financial Skills to Everyday Leasing

So now that you have a financial calculator, how do keystrokes and calculations translate into everyday leasing activities? They are integral, because every lease investment—the tenant improvements, brokerage commission, and architectural fees—are loans of a sort, extended over the period of the lease term. Because of the time value of money, you attribute an interest rate to your lease investment and amortize that over the term of the lease.

All buildings have a pro forma rent—that is, the rent that covers the cost of the property (mortgage, insurance, etc.) with some assumed leasing expenses. Any leasing costs in excess of these amounts are typically amortized on top of the rental rate.

Becoming proficient with these calculations allows leasing personnel to toggle rent terms up and down, as the parties negotiate the financial terms.

KNOW THESE FINANCIAL CALCULATOR ABBREVIATIONS

☐ PV: present value

☐ NPV: net present value

☐ FV: future value

☐ N: number of compounding periods in the calculation

☐ i: interest

☐ PMT: payment

AMORTIZING LOANS

Scenario: expressing tenant improvements (or any other landlord investment) as a function of rent.

Assume that your building is offering a suite as is with no tenant improvement allowance. Your prospective tenant loves the suite but wants funds to customize the space. You agree, saying you can, in effect, loan the tenant the improvement funds over the course of the lease term and will build it into the rent. (This scenario would also apply to any additional funds in the deal, over and above the financial package the landlord initially offers.)

You can calculate a monthly payment for every dollar of tenant improvements (or other contributions) and see its effect on the rent amount. For example, for every additional $1 in tenant improvements that the landlord contributes to a five-year lease term at 5 percent interest, how much is the monthly rate per rentable square foot increased?

KEYSTROKES

☐   Clear any numbers stored in the registers from prior calculations.

☐   Enter the 5% annual interest, expressed on a monthly basis.

☐   Enter the term length of 5 years, expressed on a monthly basis.

☐   Enter the present value: 1 ($1 per square foot).

☐   Solve for payment (PMT; obtains the payment, expressed on a monthly basis).

    (Display should read -.02, meaning that for every $1.00 per square foot of tenant improvements, the rent increases by $0.02 per square foot on a monthly basis, or $0.23 per square foot per year.)

DETERMINING NET PRESENT VALUE

Scenario: calculating a lease termination fee.

Suppose your tenant decides to relocate its business to another state and asks about terminating the lease early. There is one year left remaining on the lease term.

Calculate the net present value (NPV) of the following cash flow over the next twelve months with a discount rate of 5 percent.

Because the keystrokes vary slightly among financial calculators, the best resource for the exact keystrokes is the handbook that accompanies your calculator. But, as an overall look at what you're solving for, see below.

•   Enter the number of payment months: 12

•   Enter the discount rate: 5%

•   Enter the payment amounts (the rental amounts by month)

•   Solve for NPV

And, if you enter into discussions to lower the interest rate for the lease termination fee, you can calculate that

Online Loan Calculator

For an easy-to-use amortization calculator, go to www.decisionaide.com and click on
"Custom Loan Schedules" to access the tool.

scenario. It's easy to change the interest rate *i*, and leave
the cash flows as previously entered. Then, you can calculate the NPV. Note that the NPV will increase as the discount rate decreases.

Amortization tables typically calculate a payment at
the end of the month. To ensure your calculator is set in
this manner press *g* then *end*. Pressing *g* then *beg* will calculate the amortization payment at the beginning of the
month. Also, if you do not receive payments in any particular month, you must enter these as *0 (zero)* in order to
note the passage of a period of time, even if no payment is
made.

CALCULATING CAPITALIZATION RATES

Consider a commercial office building with, for simplici-
ty's sake, $100,000 annual net operating income in a mar-
ket with 5 percent cap rates.

$100,000 divided by .05 equals $2,000,000 estimated
market value.

Consider the impact of rising capitalization rates. If
cap rates rise by one percentage point to 6 percent, the
same building loses over 16 percent of its value. The owner
would need to increase net operating income by $20,000
(or a 20 percent increase in net operating income) in order
to achieve the same building value. That's a whole lot more

Read, Baby, Read

Up your financial literacy with a subscription to the *Wall Street Journal*, either old school via paper or online. A column titled "What's News" organizes "Business & Finance" and "World-Wide" topics on the front page. Supplemental online industry articles and discussions are also available in the *Wall Street Journal*'s real estate-focused columns.

rent or added efficiency with reduced expenses on the operating side.

Request Tenant's Information

Financial meltdowns underscore what prudent real estate professionals already know: a creditworthy tenant is golden. Assuming there are prospective tenants in the marketplace, a landlord focuses on credit checks and financial statements.

CREDIT CHECKS

For a nominal fee, landlords can ask for a prospective tenant's consent and information to run a credit check, and focus on a tenant's history of timely payments. Late or insufficient payments to other vendors, even if tenants have paid their rent on time, indicate default tendencies. Companies such as Dun & Bradstreet will provide a credit report and break down that information into late payments,

Check It Out
In addition to online and printed financial analysis resources, organizations such as the Appraisal Institute and Dun & Bradstreet's customer learning center offer classes and webinars focused on tenant credit analysis.

non-payments, vendor type, and so on. It's a fee well spent. The timing for a credit check depends on your take on the tenant. For example, you might request a credit check for some companies prior to investing space planning dollars, while you might wait until the proposal stage to verify a seemingly robust company. There's more discussion on the delicate art of timing below.

The Power of Search

In addition to obtaining a formal credit report, you can do your own online search. Fortunately, our information age places public financial information and news reports a click away. News subscription services such as LexisNexis (and similar companies) compile all sorts of media and other information on companies. And your own online search not only allows you to gain valuable information on a company, but may also provide valuable information about the principals, their interests, and peripheral news that can assist you in your leasing efforts.

A FIRSTHAND VISIT

Some real estate professionals visit the tenant in its current leased space for a firsthand look at the company's vibrancy. Personal visits can give you valuable leasing information as you watch an active sales force at work (or not), see deliveries (or not), and hear a bustling office (or not). For example, suppose a representative from a three-person office seeks to lease 5,000 square feet. That should set off warning bells and prompt a realistic discussion of the tenant's business plan to ensure its business justifies such an expansion. Let the tenant know you'd love to stop by in order to get a sense of the existing office layout to prepare for the space planning meeting. You can do double duty with the visit—look at the office configuration and assess the business's vitality. It's all part of conducting some due diligence.

FINANCIAL STATEMENTS

Trying to assess a tenant's credit as early as possible—without burdening the prospect—forestalls leasing risks and problems. As a general note, the further your lease negotiations progress, the more pressing the need to review financial information. As with so many aspects of leasing, timing matters. When financials are requested too early, prospective tenants may be alienated before they have developed any relationship with the landlord and property. Asked too late, the landlord and tenant have already invested time and (possibly) money in the transaction, making it difficult to walk away from the deal, even when credit is risky or financials don't pencil. The following is a rough timing guide of what to ask for when, as tempered by your own instincts, judgment, and company counsel.

In addition, recognize that the burden of providing financial reports varies by company. For example, a publicly held company can readily deliver audited statements while a privately held company may need more time and effort to produce the same information.

When to Ask

During the initial broker contact or touring stage, try to obtain a loose understanding of the tenant's credit from the broker or tenant. While you might avoid a direct question on credit rating during the tour, use that meeting to scout the tenant's length of time in business, occupancy length at other buildings, square footage, type of business, and clients. In a hot market with little supply, all bets are off—landlords may require financial statements at the same time as the tour.

Prior to space planning, most landlords request formal financial statements (unless the market is very soft, with tremendous space availability). In the event you proceed with space planning and its associated costs, some landlords ask prospective tenants to indemnify them for space planning expenses if the tenants do not deliver financials later or misrepresent their financial strength. (Refer to chapter 6 on space planning for more discussion.)

At the proposal stage, it's advisable to have financial statements. In the event that landlords proceed without such statements, they add a contingency clause to the proposal, dependent—among other items—on a review and approval of the tenant's financials.

It would seem foolhardy to sign a lease without a comprehensive review and approval of the tenant's financials and creditworthiness. Enough said.

What to Ask

To obtain a rounded look at your prospective tenant's financial strength, request audited financial statements for the past three years, including a balance sheet, income statement, and cash flow statement. (More on how to interpret these below.)

Contingent Upon Review

Standard proposals to lease typically contain contingency clauses for review and approval of the tenant's financials, among other items. You should confer with your own legal counsel, but many leasing representatives use some version of this statement:

> This proposal represents a preliminary outline of proposed business terms, and both parties understand and agree that no binding contract shall exist until the lease agreement has been fully executed by your client and us. This proposal shall not be considered a reservation of the premises and is subject to prior lease of all or any portion of the premises.

Upon receipt of the financials, you can send a follow-up letter to the prospective tenant confirming you have received the financials and that the decision to enter into a lease agreement will be based on that information. That way, there's some recourse should the tenant misrepresent its financial strength or history. The last thing you want is to be saddled with a tenant that moves in and defaults on the lease terms. Case law, particularly in pro-tenant states

> **Keep It Contingent**
> Standard proposals to lease typically contain contingency clauses for review and approval of the tenant's financials.

such as California, makes remedy or eviction an arduous process.

Next, confirm that the financials you receive match the signatory entity on the lease contract. In markets rife with start-up companies, you may be given financial information for a parent company instead of the subsidiary, or for a separate company that is an investor, but not an owner, on the lease. Brokers sometimes fail to differentiate between the entities, so the landlord needs to confirm that the lease signature block matches the entity represented on the financial statements.

I once lost a tenant to a competitor's building. I ruminated. I lost sleep. The tenant was a start-up, bankrolled by a major communications company. Fast-forward a few months to when the start-up defaulted at the competitor's building. The other landlord pursued legal remedies. Whoops. It turned out the big daddy communications firm was only an investor with no legal responsibility for the start-up, including the lease contract. The incident taught me a valuable lesson: absent another guarantor, the entity that signs the lease is responsible for the rent. That seems obvious, but it's easy to confuse players in the hurly-burly of a deal. From that point forward, I made sure our lease signature

blocks exactly matched the entity that had pro-
vided the financials (on which we based the deal).
Sometimes, the best deal is the one you don't do.

Foreign-Owned Entities

In an increasingly global market, you may lease to for-
eign-owned companies. These situations pose an added
challenge when verifying creditworthiness and understanding a company's ownership structure. Some landlords
require that the prospective tenant have enough United
States–based financial accounts and assets to ensure rent
payment and for collateral in the event the tenant defaults.
The *Commercial Lease Law Insider*, an industry newsletter that focuses on legal lease issues, advises that any
lease guarantor be US based.[2] Presumably any prospective tenant whose financials lead the landlord to request a
guaranty is riskier, and the landlord needs to ensure reasonable access to funds.

Book Club, Part 2

John A. Tracy's *How to Read a Financial
Report* is a short, sweet, and highly useful book that focuses on financial statement
analysis.

Evaluate Financial Statements: The Good, the Bad, and the Ugly

While you rely on accountants and analysts to dissect the financial statements used to evaluate a tenant's credit, you should also understand reports enough to make informed leasing decisions and justify the deal offered.

AUDITED, REVIEWED, AND COMPILED

Traditional financial information is conveyed via an income statement, cash flow statement, and balance sheet, and supplemented with a credit report. In addition to having an industry standard language and format, these reports—if prepared by a CPA—adhere to GAAP (generally accepted accounting principles). The uniformity assures us that a certified professional has examined the reports and that the information is conveyed in a consistent manner across reports.

> **According to New York–based accountants Grassi & Co., "Since the landscape is changing, it is important to understand the significant differences between these levels of services— Compilation, Review and Audit."**

There are varying levels of scrutiny and rigor applied to the production of financial statements. According to New York–based accountants Grassi & Co., "Since the landscape is changing, it is important to understand the significant differences between these levels of services– Compilation, Review and Audit."[3] For leasing purposes, audited reports are optimal because of the higher level of

Do You Know These Accounting Terms?

GAAP: generally accepted accounting principles

CPA: certified public accountant

AUDITED STATEMENTS: the highest level of assurance by a CPA that financials are accurate

REVIEWED: a middle level of scrutiny, limited assurance by a CPA that financials are accurate

COMPILED: assembled financial statements, CPA expresses no assurance

scrutiny and approval. Then, in order of descending preference, reviewed and compiled reports might be acceptable. In-house statements are just that, and are therefore less desirable because of the lack of an objective, third-party, qualified review. As a note, securities laws demand that all publicly held companies provide annual audited financial statements.

So what type of reports should you request from your prospective tenant? Remember the acronym BIC: balance sheet, income statement, and cash flow statement. Financial statements reflecting the past three years provide a good overview. Together, these reports offer a snapshot of current finances as well as a longer-term economic view of the company.

Remember BIC

Ask prospective tenants for Balance sheets, Income statements, and Cash flow statements for the past three years.

THE BALANCE SHEET

The balance sheet profiles a business's financial strength at a specific moment in time, usually at the close of an accounting period. It details material and intangible items the business owns (assets) and money the business owes—credit to creditors (liabilities) and owners (shareholders' equity). Balance sheets contain standard categories of assets, liabilities, and net worth.

Assets include cash, merchandise inventory, land and buildings, equipment, machinery, furniture, patents, trademarks, and so on, as well as money due from individuals or other businesses (accounts or notes receivable).

Liabilities are funds acquired for a business via loans or the sale of property or services to the business on credit. Creditors acquire promissory notes to be paid at a designated future date but do not own any portion of the business. Other liabilities, such as litigation or environmental issues, may not be visible.

Shareholders' net worth (or capital) is money invested into a business by the owners for the business's use.

THE INCOME STATEMENT

The second primary report included in a company's financial statement is the statement of income, a measurement of a company's sales, expenses, and net income or loss over a specific period of time. Income statements are prepared at regular intervals to show the results of operating during those accounting periods. It follows GAAP and contains specific revenue and expense categories regardless of the nature of the business.

THE CASH FLOW STATEMENT

The cash flow statement reveals where cash comes from and how it is used for a given period of time. Leasing personnel use this statement to identify items such as deficiencies in collecting receivables, unrealistic trade credit, or loan repayment schedules. The statement also identifies surplus that can be invested on a short-term basis or used to reduce debt.

The cash flow statement also reveals how much cash has been internally generated from sales and the collection of accounts receivable and how much has been borrowed from external sources. External sources may include borrowing from financial institutions as well as ownership investment in the business. The uses of cash generally fall into three separate categories: distributions (dividends) to owners, capital expenditures, and reduction of debt.

ANALYZING RATIOS

Operating ratios are benchmarking tools that allow us to see how the company under review stacks up against other companies in similar lines of business. Over time, ratios tell a longitudinal story with trends. These ratios inform leasing decisions as you assess risk and decide how much capital to invest in a deal.

> **Operating ratios are benchmarking tools that allow us to see how the company under review stacks up against other companies in similar lines of business.**

While ratios vary from industry to industry as well as geographically, landlords want assurance that the tenant can pay rent. To that end, landlords examine the rent coverage ratio, that is, how much the rent (or projected rent) is expected to cost the tenant relative to its income and other obligations.

SUMMARY OF THE TENANT'S FINANCIAL HEALTH

After running a credit check and obtaining financial reports and reviewing them, most leasing departments prepare a financial summary of the deal. A synopsis, it covers the tenant's financial strength, credit history, and type of business, and highlights any areas of financial weakness, if applicable. The summary also includes all the proposed economic points of the deal, including the important net effective rent (which takes into consideration free rent and capital lease investments). Leasing representatives circulate the summary to the building ownership prior to giving the prospective tenant a lease proposal so that any landlord objections or concerns may be addressed prior to the lease negotiation and signature.

Protect Your Downside: Defensive Leasing

What if there are some riskier aspects discovered in the tenant's financial reports, but other factors, such as a tough market or undesirable space, compel you to lease?

Leasing personnel can take a protective stance by requiring increased security deposits, letters of credit, guaranties, and prepaid rent to shore up the risk of a tenant with less than stellar financials.

SECURITY DEPOSIT

First, and perhaps most simply, leasing representatives can ask for a more substantial security deposit. This gives the landlord instant access to cash in the event of a tenant default. And companies such as funded start-up firms can be flush with cash but have little credit history. For the tenant who protests locking up a six-month security deposit, landlords sometimes agree to decrease the amount of a required security deposit over time as the tenant fulfills its lease obligation and builds a track record of timely rent payment.

LETTER OF CREDIT

Next, leasing representatives may ask for an irrevocable letter of credit from the tenant's bank so the landlord can collect rent immediately in the event of default. One step removed from instant cash (i.e., the security deposit), these letters do give the landlord a fairly easy solution in the case of default. As added solace, a bank's willingness to grant such a letter is a positive indication of the prospective tenant's creditworthiness.

I once took a memorable elevator ride with the founder and president of my firm, Bill Wilson. In between the lobby and the twentieth floor, Bill and I discussed the terms on the table for a prospective tenant. As he stepped from the elevator,

Bill announced, "Credit is king," meaning he'd do a deal all day long with a creditworthy tenant and a lower rental rate as opposed to a risker tenant at a higher rental rate. Later, after lowering the rent a bit, I landed the tenant. Over the next years as the tenant expanded and extended its lease, I remembered Bill's excellent advice. Moreover, when the booming real estate market slowed and floundering tenants fled their leases, our buildings remained relatively full with solvent tenants able to write a monthly rent check.

PREPAID RENT

A third alternative is to ask for six to twelve months of prepaid rent. Similar to an increased security deposit, this option takes away the hassle of dealing with a potential late- or non-payer of rent, but it's a fairly tough proposal to negotiate, as tenants dislike tying up their cash. An appropriate compromise might be for the landlord to discount the early rent payment in order to acknowledge the time value of money.

LEASE GUARANTY

In addition, sometimes a lease guaranty eases a landlord's jitters over the prospective tenant's financial state, if it's signed by a different entity than that on the lease (if your tenant goes belly up, a guaranty from a different entity is not swept up in bankruptcy procedures). Of course, a guaranty is only as good as the strength and liquidity of the guarantor's financials that support the promise. If the guarantor is a company, it should have US-based assets that can be accessed in the case of tenant default. And if an individual guarantees the lease, you need to consider whether that agreement could be compromised by a move, divorce, or other extenuating circumstance.

> **Leasing personnel can take a protective stance by requiring increased security deposits, letters of credit, guaranties, and prepaid rent to shore up the risk of a tenant with less than stellar financials.**

LIMITED RIGHTS FOR CREDIT-RISKY TENANTS

Leasing representatives also tinker with lease language that disallows tenant privileges if the lessee fails to meet rental obligations. For example, landlords can insert a clause into extension or expansion options that renders those options null and void if the tenant pays rent late twice during the lease term. Better yet, landlords do not give expansion or extension options to tenants with wobbly financials. And prudent landlords retain substantial late-payment and interest-charge clauses in the contract for nonpayment (or late payment) of rent so tenants have a disincentive to miss payments.

ONGOING FINANCIAL REPORTS

Yet another tool in the defensive leasing arsenal, landlords can insert lease language requiring tenants to provide audited financial statements at regular intervals or upon request during the lease term. Refer to your own legal counsel for the language.

Finally, think creatively and intelligently. It takes some work to achieve a professional comfort level with companies that have mediocre credit or are not yet profitable. Measures such as a lease guaranty, an irrevocable letter of credit, or a large security deposit should also take into account any capital investments (commissions and tenant improvements), plus several months of rent to cover leasing downtime in the event of tenant default. Defensive leasing makes good business sense in any real estate environment.

PART III

Closing the Lease Deal

CHAPTER 8

Craft a Proposal

"Strike while the iron is hot."
—*Any old blacksmith*

GOAL: CRAFT AND DELIVER A PROPOSAL
THAT WILL LEAD TO A SIGNED LEASE

In the third portion of this book, with a successful tour, space plan, and financial analysis behind you, the focus turns to presenting a winning proposal that leads to the next stage of lease negotiation and, hopefully, a fully executed lease document.

Present a Compelling Proposal

Successful proposals contain many important elements, each vitally important: good timing, an understanding of your tenant, a winning tenor and attitude, and clarity of deal terms in conjunction with deal terms (rent, tenant improvement package, rights, and concessions) that compete relative to the local market.

GOOD TIMING

Timing plays a critical role in proposals. At a certain point in the deal (after tours and space planning), the landlord and tenant are understood to be negotiating primarily with each other. Exclusive daters, the implicit or explicit understanding is that they are headed to the altar. As in romance, real estate commitment can become a little blurry around the edges. Take the space off the market too early and you lose other prospects and some negotiating leverage. Fail to commit until too late and your prospect may become jittery and bolt. So when is the right time? More art than science, superb professionals develop a sense of timing over years of experience. For mere mortals, typical right times might be when the tenant's broker says your building has made the short list, when the tenant comes back to see the building for a second or third time, when you ask if the prospect would like a proposal and the answer is yes, when the tour went so well that the tenant is eager to proceed, and so on.

I've seen deals unravel during innocent cocktail parties. Some rumor surfaces—like a company moving—and a partygoer says his brother's best friend is a broker who can get a better deal in a nearby building . . . the next day the broker calls your prospective tenant. The tenant hesitates, filled with uncertainty, and boom, momentum cools. That's why there's no time like the present to close a deal.

Conversely, flags that demonstrate a prospect's disinterest can also be reflected through timing. For instance, if more than two weeks elapse between the tour and any proposal discussion, the space (or location or rent) probably does not make sense for the tenant. If the prospect (or the broker) does not take your telephone call, or doesn't respond to a call or email within twenty-four hours, continuing on to the proposal stage becomes less likely. At the end of the day, a proposal is just that, so don't sweat the decision of the precise right moment, but do pay attention to movement and trends: forward, stagnant, and backward. After several deals, you will develop a sense of momentum.

They're Just Not That into You

Prospective tenants who are slow to return a call or email, who wait weeks to ask for a proposal (to shop it in the market), or who send a low-level employee for the space planning meeting (they are not invested in the office layout) indicate disinterest.

UNDERSTANDING YOUR PROSPECTIVE TENANT

Taking the tenant's business temperature allows you to tailor a competitive proposal. First, pay attention to what the tenant values and highlight those features of the property in the proposal. For example, let's suppose you toured a fitness fanatic whose eyes lit up when he saw the weight room available to all tenants. You might feature the fitness center and outdoor basketball court in the proposal. Then, when delivering such, you let him know about the regular pickup basketball games. Corny perhaps, but this type of interaction shows that you're the type of landlord who cares about tenants and their interests. And that mindset goes a long way in assuring tenants that your service will extend to their facility concerns.

In addition, in our technological age of text, cloud, and cell, determining the best communication method for the client helps your leasing efforts. Massachusetts Institute of Technology professor Sherry Turkle underscores the importance of strong communication by balancing electronic exchanges with face-to-face conversations that

---

**Pay Attention to Your Prospects'
(and Their Brokers') Habits**

Are they morning people? Do they stay late on Friday afternoons? Become animated after a morning swim? By keying into personal preferences through observation and conversation, you improve your chances of successful communication.

allow for deeper dialogue and nuance.[1] By learning how colleagues prefer to communicate—email, text, iMessage, meetings, and so on—you can improve your level of service to prospective tenants and brokers. Of course, certain documents, such as proposals, need to be written, but the communication around and delivery of formal documents can be adjusted for your client.

STRIKING A WINNING TENOR AND ATTITUDE

The proposal stage perches the landlord in a delicate position between courtship and commitment. The tenant is, oh, so attractive. Yet, you still want to be sure you can strike a good rent deal with an acceptable level of capital investment. This strange dance of letting tenants know you want them while simultaneously outlining lease obligations has a seesaw movement. While this phase of leasing requires dialogue and compromise, you need to keep your eyes on the prize: a long-term, strong landlord-tenant relationship. As computer scientist and author Randy Pausch observed, "Brick walls are there to give us a chance to show how badly we want something."[2] Allowing the goal of winning the prospective tenant to underpin all of your discussions makes negotiations more workable. Thus, framing your proposal in a positive manner communicates your intended goal: to welcome the prospect as a tenant.

Recognizing Potential Tension

In order to handle conflict, today's literature lauds persistence as a critical ingredient of success. In researching success, both psychologists and business professors zero in on resilience, the ability to recover from or adjust to change or plain bad luck. The term *adversity quotient* (AQ) has gained traction in business nomenclature. As a result, many MBA programs incorporate AQ theory courses into their curriculums. Indeed, Stanford University's Resilience Project states that setbacks should be considered "bona fide revenue through which new perspectives are gained and critical shifts in thinking are heralded."[3] Persistence and resilience seem worthwhile habits to cultivate, especially because real estate is a long-term business with tenants gained and, sometimes, lost.

> *My company CEO believed that those frightened of conflict would not succeed in real estate leasing. While every property manager and leasing agent may not have the iron stomach of a litigator, encountering some level of conflict seems inevitable. Multiple parties, different economic goals, and long-term commitments create a certain degree of potential strife. For those who avoid conflict, it can be tough to iron out differences and close a lease deal. The good news is that, in my experience, once the negotiation points are resolved, the lease signed, and the tenant moved in, it's full steam ahead. Short-term memory can be a beautiful thing.*

A Clear Proposal

USE AN INTRODUCTORY SUMMARY TO HIGHLIGHT YOUR PROPERTY

A proposal's brevity can be deceptive. Although just a few pages long, proposals contain all the financial terms and important rights of a lease. These business points provide the infrastructure on which the remainder of the lease document will hang, so they need to be thorough.

Open your proposal with a description of the property, its amenities, and so on, with an overview similar to the property introduction you used on the tour. Seemingly redundant, the summary assists the tenant, particularly any decision-making executives who have not yet toured the site or specific suite. In addition, this transmittal gives leasing personnel an opportunity to reiterate the attributes of the property, rather than relying on others to communicate such.

To pave the way for ensuing business terms discussions, thoughtful landlords express how much they look forward to welcoming the prospect as a tenant and to a continued, strong relationship.

OFFERING BUSINESS TERMS

A proposal contains most of the quantifiable elements of a lease: the rentable square footage, rent, term length, tenant improvements, brokerage acknowledgment (if any), security deposit, operating expense obligation, rights such as expansion or extension, parking spaces, storage space, and a contingency clause that clarifies there's no deal until the lease is fully signed and delivered to each party.

BUSINESS TERMS THAT ARE USUALLY SPECIFIED IN A PROPOSAL TO LEASE

- ☐ Rentable square footage
- ☐ Rent
- ☐ Term length
- ☐ Tenant improvements
- ☐ Parties to the lease (defining specific landlord and tenant)

☐ Commission (not necessarily the amount but the acknowledgment that a commission will be paid to a named brokerage firm)

☐ Security deposit

☐ Operating expense obligation

☐ Parking spaces

☐ Storage space (if applicable)

☐ Rights such as those to expand, extend, terminate, or relocate

☐ A contingency clause that says the terms of the proposal are not binding until the lease is signed

LEASE RIGHTS AND CONCESSIONS

Whether you manage tenant space rights electronically or on paper, here's a word to the wise: double-check the existing rights on any space before offering it to another prospect.

Because most encumbrance clauses specify that the rent (and other general business terms of the deal) the landlord will offer to the new tenant needs to be congruent with the existing tenant's—oftentimes within 90–95 percent—you need to know that the proposal terms are within this margin before you formally notify the existing tenant of the offer. Should a deal evolve to be outside of these parameters, the landlord might need to restart the entire notice process.

To further complicate matters, most rights of first refusal have a response time of three to five days (and ten days, in some instances). This waiting period—after the space has been offered but before the tenant is obligated to respond—can cool a landlord's leasing efforts in the market. So, in order to start the clock ticking, landlords often offer the space to the existing tenant prior to doling out a proposal to another prospect, but only after the prospect

Electronic Stacking Plans

Software programs that track existing tenant rights (by displaying spaces with colors, ticklers for expirations, and important notification dates, etc.) can prevent proposal errors such as offering space without notifying an existing tenant who has a right on the same space.

has become somewhat serious (otherwise, the landlord has to send a notice every time a prospect tours the space).

Be Parsimonious with Rights

As you can see, managing rights becomes a cumbersome process, which is why landlords prefer not to concede them easily. When a tenant requests a right, the landlord can counter by giving examples of tenants who have expanded sans formal lease rights. Although this scenario may seem one-sided, the reality is that by encumbering space, the landlord limits his ability to accommodate growing and new tenants. In general, landlords are motivated to satisfy existing tenant renewals and expansions—they're less costly, they require less paperwork, and the credit risk is already known.

When a tenant insists on such rights, size matters. Typically, the more square footage a tenant leases, the more willing a landlord is to grant rights and other special concessions.

In addition, the type of right you give makes a difference. Typically, there's a right of offer, a right of first (or second) refusal, a right to expand into a specific space, and so on. Understanding the nuances between these various rights is helpful. (More discussion on this in chapter 10)

THE CONTINGENCY CLAUSE

Most proposals contain a contingency clause that specifies that the proposal is not a reservation of the premises and is also dependent on the review and approval of the tenant's financial statements. Be sure to ask your legal counsel about this important clause. (See appendixes C and D for examples of lease proposals for both new and existing tenants, but note that they are intended as reference only. You should review your own lease proposal with your legal counsel.)

> *I once had a broker go absolutely ballistic with me over the telephone. He swore. He yelled. Why? He claimed he hadn't understood that the offered space was contingent on an existing tenant's renewal, even though we'd included such a clause in the proposal. While the broker may have blamed us to avoid embarrassment in front of his client, I realized I could have done better. I could have personally told the broker that the space was hot and that we were negotiating with others too. Then, he could have relayed the news to his client. Or at least he would have known and been able to decide what to do with that information. I resolved that in the future, I would have a conversation with the broker in addition to emailing or mailing a proposal with the written contingency clause.*

Present the Proposal

When the proposal is complete, imitate your local florist and make the delivery in person. Arrange a convenient time, letting the broker and/or tenant know you'd like a few minutes to review the proposal with them. This face-to-face meeting allows you to explain the proposal, address any questions, and, most importantly, gauge the tenant's and broker's reactions. While brokers are accustomed to maintaining a poker face, over time you will develop a feel for the proposal response based on comments, body language, type of questions, and so on. If, however, brokers and tenants can't meet or geography limits you, one approach is to let the broker know you are emailing (or mailing) the proposal, and then set up a videoconference chat or telephone call for review. Ultimately, a smoother proposal delivery saves time.

While our busy lives may tempt us to just press the Send button, prepping your proposal delivery with a call to arrange a review minimizes confusion. Calling ahead is of the utmost importance if a proposal contains variances from prior discussions, expectations, or potential misunderstandings. Few business people like surprises, especially the ones that lighten their wallets. For instance, if you are going to require a hefty letter of credit for a start-up company, it's best to let the tenant and broker know in advance of the proposal delivery. When a proposal arrives but is incongruent with prior discussions and interactions, tenants get nervous. Understandably, the tenants wonder what other surprises await them. Bam! There you are, with a skeptical—or worse, distrustful—tenant before even digging into the meat of negotiations.

The tenant's feedback, whether spoken or expressed via body language, will give you clues as to what points might be contested. In most cases, prospective tenants will focus on and ask questions about the issues most important to them. Pay attention to these points because during negotiations, it's helpful to understand a tenant's priorities.

One developer told me that, early in his career, he invited a client to a baseball game. After the seventh inning, things were going so well that the developer produced a folded lease from his back pocket and his client signed it. Lucky? Sure. Prepared? You bet. Sometimes relationship building does produce great in-the-moment opportunities on which an organized leasing agent can capitalize. Most of the time, however, social events are just that. Focus on the rapport, and the deal will likely come (but it doesn't hurt to hope for the best and be prepared!).

Follow Up on the Proposal

CLARIFYING

After reviewing the proposal (hopefully in person), follow up with the broker or tenant in one to two business days. Again, keeping the momentum of the deal going allows progress. If a prospective tenant stalls when responding to the proposal, it may indicate apathy about the property or possibly a slow decision-making process within the company. Ask the broker when the prospect plans to respond with a written counterproposal, so you can schedule time for review.

In my twenty-year career, I have had a prospective tenant sign and return a proposal without negotiating any of its terms, once. That's right, once. I practically fell out of my chair. So I consider the proposal a starting point from which we'll discuss and settle on terms. Usually, a two-round session gets us to agreed-upon business points. From there, the tenant is ready to review the lease document. And when too much time elapses between proposal discussions, I know the deal has gone cold. The prospect may be negotiating more earnestly with another building, isn't serious about moving, or has a dysfunctional decision-making process.

MAINTAINING MOMENTUM

During the proposal and follow-up stages, let the tenant know the building and your time are in demand. For instance, you might tell the tenant, "I want to be sure I have allotted time on my calendar to discuss your important proposal. Do you have time Wednesday morning from nine to ten?" In this way, you lend a sense of urgency and efficiency to the process and communicate that, while desired, the tenant is not the only fish in the sea. By keeping up the momentum, you are able to move on to the next deal phase: negotiation.

CHAPTER 9

Negotiate a Deal

"I think of real estate as a little bit like cooking or like art."[1]
–*Jerry Speyer, founder Tishman Speyer*

GOAL: EXAMINE VARIOUS NEGOTIATION APPROACHES, STYLES, AND TECHNIQUES TO REACH AGREEMENT ON PROPOSAL TERMS AND PROGRESS TO LEASE DOCUMENTATION

In order to close a lease deal, you'll need to wind your way through a maze of negotiations. Prized by flinty labor leaders and diplomats alike, negotiation skills are considered a core competency for nearly any profession today. Conflict is "an inevitable—and useful—part of life,"[2] according to author Roger Fisher, coauthor of the iconic book, *Getting to Yes*. If you are frightened of conflict and the chaos that can accompany negotiations, you might settle for avoidance in exchange for concessions. Instead, you can strive to embrace a new process that maximizes potential solutions in a respectful manner, while accepting that you will encounter turmoil and disagreement along the way. In the process, you'll need to cultivate your own best negotiation style, suited to your temperament and personality strengths.

Adopt an Approach to Negotiation

START WITH A MINDSET

Setting expectations may be exactly what you need to cross the finish line. According to Dr. Alex Lickerman, author of *The Undefeated Mind*, data shows that expectations determine our perception of the difficulty of a task.[3] So, by anticipating obstacles, you can take the expected challenges in stride. Conversely, when you foresee an unencumbered path, any stone might throw you for a loop, resulting in your own early defeat. By reframing your perspective, you perceive negotiation as a natural phase of lease transactions that will require constructive problem-solving. Yes, deals can steal our sleep, but a revised mindset helps us leap the hurdle of negotiations.

> *I heard an anecdote about an Olympian who, when he went home to the snowy Midwest, slept naked with the windows open and without blankets. His rationale? He trained for pain. The athlete theorized that his competitors might not be accustomed to such high levels of discomfort. By exposing himself to bitterly harsh environments, he earned an advantage.*

The same theory might apply to leasing (or any difficult task in life). Ironically, acknowledging— and expecting—a certain inevitable level of hardship can ease a journey.

CONSIDER YOUR STYLE

The way in which individuals express their signature style depends largely on temperament. Susan Cain, author of *Quiet*, discusses the power of understanding and utilizing your own negotiating style. Cain explains that extroverts—articulate, sure-footed, and sometimes loud— tend to shoot from the hip. In contrast, introverts tend to prepare well and ask questions that tease out solutions.[4] For example, an introvert that has prepared well can use a modulated, even voice to diffuse emotions and present a deal that appears logical and fair. The exuberant extrovert, on the other hand, might announce recent fitness center upgrades and emphasize how much the landlord looks forward to a long-term relationship with the prospect. For practice in developing your own style, try role-playing a proposal with a colleague. Cain says the question of temperament—where we fall on the introvert-extrovert spectrum—dictates our preferences and that both can work. The point is to recognize your own style so you can play to its strengths.

> **Cain explains that extroverts— articulate, sure-footed, and sometimes loud—tend to shoot from the hip. In contrast, introverts tend to prepare well and ask questions that tease out solutions.**

Regardless of your temperament, as in other arenas of life, those who manage their emotions fare well. According to Gary Noesner, chief negotiator for the FBI for ten years, many personalities can be good at problem-solving "but one of the universal attributes that we see is self-control"[5] in negotiators who "don't get flustered or react to events in a highly emotional way."[6] Calming yourself allows physiology to work at its creative best because your brain can explore solutions rather than contend with the fight-or-flight sensation that overwhelming emotions can create. As a bonus, it's just more pleasant to work with someone under emotional control.

I know a sly cat who placed an orange and black penholder from Princeton University on his desk, facing guests. Although he did not attend the Ivy League institution, he insinuated he had. Business has all types—the posers, the outrageous, the honest. It's important to maintain a sense of humor and perspective, especially when working with some of these characters.

Preparing for Successful Negotiations

Now that you expect some disruption, how do you better solve the inevitable conflicts over price, tenant improvements, and lease clauses? Let's start with the basics.

IDENTIFY THE DECISION MAKERS

When discussing lease terms, identify the appropriate decision makers and negotiators; debating terms with unauthorized personnel is a waste of time. One way to avoid confusion is to ask prospective tenants to describe their lease negotiation and signing processes. Whoever has the right to sign the lease is a decision maker, although there are likely others as well. A contact who won't actually sign the lease but is responsible for concluding the process also has decision-making authority. By confirming that you are indeed negotiating with the appropriate parties, you avoid stalemates and delays.

> *I once sat in a conference room alongside a land-lord who was meeting with the anchor tenant of a large office park. Flanked by three beefy men, the petite tenant representative stood barely five feet tall in heels. During the meeting, the landlord directed his comments to the men. I watched the woman become annoyed. I left the room, ostensibly to take a phone call, and scribbled a note, "Annie is the lead negotiator. Talk to her." I then returned to the room and handed the folded "telephone" mes-sage to the landlord. He cringed and redirected his attention, thereby salvaging the deal. It's important to speak to the decision maker.*

SET THE RIGHT TIME

Be conscientious when scheduling negotiation times. For instance, avoid lunchtime or end-of-the-day-talks that might result in a difficult commute for others, and be aware of the differences in time zones. Studies show that the hour before lunch (when hunger strikes) and the late afternoon (when fatigue occurs) can be cantankerous negotiating times. Negotiations are tough enough without imposing the added stresses of hunger, fatigue, and loom-ing commute traffic.

> ### Draw a Boundary
>
> Focus conference calls and meetings by setting a time deadline and agenda. For example, saying, "I've scheduled the conference call for 45 minutes," helps attendees focus on the issues at hand.

LET'S GET PHYSICAL

Pay attention to your physical setting and cues, so as to encourage cooperation rather than competition.

Seating Arrangements

Negotiators typically take sides on opposite sides of the table, literally and figuratively. Fisher suggests that negotiating parties sit side by side to encourage collaboration as parties seek to settle concerns. A desk that separates the parties, a chair that sits higher than the others, and cold room temperatures all conspire to create an environment where conflict may be exacerbated. Instead, use equal seating and a comfortable room to encourage joint problem-solving.[7]

One of San Francisco's leading asset managers relayed his secret formula for interviewing potential employees. He places the interviewee's chair close to a large, leafy plant in the corner of his office. If an interviewee sits down and bats palm fronds from his head he's a no-go. However, if the interviewee adjusts the chair forward (and out of

the plant's reach), he progresses to a second inter-
view. Why? Well, the executive considers negotia-
tion, which includes physical awareness, a critical
facet of the job. The test evaluates one's recognition
and correction of compromised situations.

Stand Up Straight and Look 'Em in the Eye

Mom was right when she told you eye contact indicates confidence, connection, and respect. A *Wall Street Journal* article reports that people should be making eye contact 60–70 percent of the time to create an emotional connection, with a feel-good gaze lasting seven to ten seconds.[8] Any shorter and you may be dismissive; longer and you may border on creepy. Typical poor habits include lacking steady eye contact, gazing downward at a table or at notes while in a meeting, staring intensely into others' eyes, or worse, making eye contact while typing a text message or doing something else at the same time. In a world of flashing lights and pinging notifications, personal connection—primarily conveyed through eye contact—has become increasingly important.

Once again, temperament plays a role in how you (literally) see others. For instance, introverts may gaze into space, not because they are distracted, but because others may speak in a too-loud voice. And boisterous extroverts with their dominating gazes may unnerve listeners. Those who want to modify their presentation habits often videotape themselves, hire a business coach or corporate trainer, or participate in groups such as Toastmasters.

FOCUS ON BUSINESS TERMS FIRST

Most landlords and tenants settle business (i.e., financial) terms before ironing out the remainder of the contractual lease language. The beauty of financial terms is that they can be quantified, which allows you to know more precisely what you are trading with each negotiation. Leasing business terms include rent, term lengths, operating expenses, security deposits, tenant improvements, insurance requirements, commissions, and any other monetary inducements or concessions. Other important issues such as signage, parking, extension and expansion rights, and so on may not explicitly entail dollars but can affect the financial profile of the deal. While the real estate industry often focuses on face rent, the truth is that the net value of a lease is a function of *all* the economic terms of a deal, as discussed earlier.

The period of negotiating business terms is fairly short, usually a function of tenant size and lease complexity. Smaller leases can be negotiated in a few weeks (or sooner) while large suites with a national firm might take up to several months because of the bureaucracy involved. In tight markets, the demand for space creates its own urgency to come to deal terms in short order. In a market with excess space supply, landlords sometimes create their own deadlines to expedite an agreement.

Know Your Amortized Capital Investment

With a financial analysis of the proposed lease, you can tie every added dollar of capital investment per square foot to an amortized x dollars at a certain interest rate over the lease term. This one-to-one correspondence allows you to make appropriate trade-offs. For example, $1.00 per square foot amortized over five years at a 5 percent interest rate equates to $0.23 per square foot per year. So for every dollar contributed to tenant improvements (or other capital expenditures), the landlord would have to raise the rent by $0.23 per square foot per year. Understanding and calculating these numbers allows you to have an informed negotiation discussion such as the following example.

Sample Script

Assume the landlord has already proposed a rent including tenant improvements per an approved space plan. The conversation about lease terms might go something like this:

> **Tenant:** I'd like to add glass sidelights to our offices and be sure our carpet is free of any adhesives or chemicals.
> **Landlord:** I should mention that our building-standard carpet is installed over pad rather than with adhesive glue and that the new carpet will be aired out for several days via operable suite windows. Now, let's talk about these proposed change orders. Say you choose to install Shaw's Green with Envy carpet tiles; those will add $3,500 to our existing tenant improvement allowance. And if you want to buy three more sidelights, those total $3,500. We (the landlord) have the available funds, so if you want these upgrades, we can amortize this over your five-year lease term, and the rent will increase by $132 per month. Would you like to adjust the rent this way?

> **Tenant:** We definitely want the sidelights (at $3,500). I guess the standard carpet is fine because it's a good quality.
> **Landlord:** With the sidelights only, the rent increases by $66 a month.
> **Tenant:** We can live with that.

The same scenario applies to concessions with more free rent or other out-of-pocket expenses that are above the landlord's pro forma rent and inducement package. This quantifiable way of negotiating clarifies discussions so that additional capital costs correspond to rental hikes. By delineating and quantifying the choices and changes, the tenant and landlord make informed decisions.

KEEP YOUR PRIORITIES STRAIGHT

Leasing negotiations should fit the landlord's priorities for that property. For instance, one property owner may value long-term tenants while another wants full building occupancy, even with month-to-month leases. Or a landlord may value high contract (i.e., face) rents, knowing the building will be sold within the next two years. In addition, a landlord might prefer a certain tenant mix, such as accounting or legal firms, knowing that symbiotic businesses, such as notaries, temporary staffing firms, and insurance companies, create a vertical hierarchy of sorts within the property. Knowing and focusing on the landlord's financial bottom line and priorities allows you to negotiate with clarity and confidence.

Broker as Consultant

Occasionally, a landlord and prospective tenant develop a rapport and converse directly, without the broker's involvement. This arrangement can arise because the broker feels comfortable with the landlord, the tenant is an existing one, the logistics of coordinating all parties slow the deal to an ineffective pace, and so on. Still later, once the economic points of a lease are agreed upon, some brokers step aside to let the landlord and tenant complete the discussions and documentation. Conscientious landlords copy brokers on marked-up lease copies and other correspondence. In addition, they let brokers know when execution copies of documents are distributed, so that the brokers may assist in expediting signatures. Depending on the broker and the tenant, this type of relationship can streamline negotiations to bring the lease to a close.

Understanding Some Negotiation Fundamentals

PRESERVE THE RELATIONSHIP BUT DO WHAT'S FAIR

The classic book *Getting to Yes* by Fisher, Ury, and Patton is based on work by the Harvard Negotiation Project, a group that deals with conflict resolution, from everyday contracts to international diplomatic discussions. The Harvard Negotiation Project invokes the phrase *principled negotiations* to describe a process that "decides issues based on their merits rather than through a haggling process."[9] The group espouses looking for common ground and then, in the areas of discord, relying on objective standards rather than personal ones. The notion of principled negotiations also means that you don't place yourself at the whim of every personality involved, but rather that you approach your discussions with a calm, thoughtful plan in order to reach an agreement. The first task is to separate the people from the problem. Once you have acknowledged personal interest and emotion, you can focus on your respective concerns rather than individual positions. Next, you brainstorm for solutions to your issues. Finally, you engage objective criteria to resolve the outstanding issues.

Negotiations that are "hard on the merits, soft on the people"[10] work well, according to authors Fisher, Ury, and Patton. The emotions and temperaments that individuals bring to the table make every negotiation unique. For example, a property manager may acknowledge, "I know you have been upset at the recent noise level from the building renovation, but let's see how that may benefit you. We have the ability to offer you expanded signage, and the elevators operate much more quickly now." By recognizing and acknowledging this human element, Fisher explains that parties are then able to concentrate on solving the problem in a more collaborative fashion.

> **Negotiations that are "hard on the merits, soft on the people" work well, according to authors Fisher, Ury, and Patton.**

Fisher emphasizes the importance of focusing on concerns and interests, rather than entanglement into stubborn positions that one feels compelled to defend merely because one has taken a stance. Otherwise, compromise can be seen as capitulation. Fisher draws an analogy to splitting an orange. Conventional wisdom holds that splitting the fruit in half works. However, if one party wants the

Getting to Yes: Four Crucial Negotiation Steps

PEOPLE: Separate the people from the problem.

INTERESTS: Focus on interests, not positions.

OPTIONS: Invent multiple options looking for mutual gains before deciding what to do.

CRITERIA: Insist that the result be based on some objective standard."[11]

pulp and the other the peel, why not hear the concerns and then address them? Clearly, one party getting the pulp and one the peel works better than simply dividing the orange in half. In this example, addressing individual concerns means a bigger win than what might have been achieved with a traditional approach.

KEEP EMOTIONS UNDER CONTROL

Deal strife seems inevitable, and although it's easier said than done, recognizing the onset of heightened tensions can forestall a crisis. Author Daniel Goleman delves into psychological changes that affect behavior. When a stimulus triggers the primal part of the brain responsible for fight-or-flight survival instincts, you become, according to Goleman, "emotionally hijacked."[12] This emotional five-alarm fire obviates our ability to think and act calmly and rationally.

Goleman reports that there is good news, though: you can learn emotional intelligence. The key is to be able to

Be the Captain of Your Own Ship

Are you irritated by a long morning commute? Are you worried about the consequences if you can't close this lease deal? Recognizing underlying feelings prevents them from influencing negotiations unduly. Self-soothing strategies, such as a minute of deep breathing or simply acknowledging peripheral feelings, can calm you enough to negotiate well.

recognize your feelings and then regulate them. Of course, that's easier said than done. Sometimes, charged emotions or adversarial personalities strain the deal-making process. In this instance, taking a break—the adult version of a time-out—diffuses tension. Consider rescheduling the lease clause review or leaving the conference room. Also, it may be helpful to enlist a neutral or congenial personality to handle an aspect of the deal. FBI negotiator Gary Noesner explains that the harder one pushes, the likelier the other party is to push back.[13] So rather than continuing a hard line of negotiation, step back and consider a range of approaches to turn down the temperature. They may include involving others, reiterating your desire to work with the tenant, or turning attention to another–less contentious–lease issue.

INVOKE THE BIG DOGS

When negotiations become heated, it can help to invoke others. Saying that a point is a deal breaker for an investor (assuming it's true), allows others to shoulder some of the responsibility for saying no. Similarly, telling the tenant that you need to seek approval from or run a point by investors can buy you time for emotions to cool when things become heated. These techniques keep the focus on content, rather than individual stances.

IDENTIFY DEAL BREAKERS

Ah, the sacred cow. Distinguishing deal-breaker points from lesser priorities is critical to leasing success. Oftentimes part of the partnership contract, loan documents, or investment strategy, deal breakers are generally known issues. Typical examples include insurance, indemnification, capital expenditure thresholds, and use restrictions. If, during the course of a negotiation, a critical issue arises, it's best to identify it as a deal breaker. Do not, however, cry wolf too often, or the prospective tenant will view your statement as a negotiating ploy rather than a legitimate concern. Wise landlords take a nonnegotiable stance only when they are willing to walk away from the deal over the issue.

Too many times, inexperienced parties assume that some aspect of the proposal is hard and fast, when only a few points may be deal breakers. That's why you should have a conversation while reviewing the proposal (instead of simply delivering the proposal). The worst-case scenario is having a tenant decline to lease based on a review of written terms only, without any dialogue. Deal breakers are usually few and far between.

There's a difference between the rigors of negotiating a deal and a stalemate that degrades a long-term relationship. If the deal has progressed past the financial review and the parties have agreed on the business terms, there's very little that can't be worked out with legal language. Still, serious unforeseen issues can arise—deal-breaker issues— that force a landlord to walk from the deal. It's heartbreaking, but it can be a prudent decision. At any rate, make the decision to walk based on reason, not just fatigue, which can set in once negotiations become difficult and lengthy.

Nearly every deal I've worked on has reached a fatigue point, when momentum stalls. Giving up seems appealing. When that happens, I think of the most effective negotiator I know, who would tell the tenant, "We're not confused—you're a great company and we want to do this deal with you." His confident expression of clear intent would soothe feelings and reinvigorate the discussions. Sometimes people appreciate reassurance.

Smoothing Over Trouble in Paradise

In the course of negotiations, you may employ some common techniques or recognize those used by others. Here are a few:

QUID PRO QUO

The Latin term *quid pro quo* means "something for something." Some leasing professionals believe it best to receive a concession for each point. For instance, you might let the tenant know why you are compromising on particular points with a comment such as, "Because we value your creditworthiness, we are willing to lower our security deposit somewhat." This discipline helps you make conscious decisions and communicate exactly what is being traded. Reciprocity is the name of the game.

At the start of negotiations, I visualize one hand extending itself while the other hand closes and pulls toward me. Somehow this image simplifies the daunting job of negotiation. It also keeps me conscious of securing something for each point I concede. And if I give a point without requiring an exchange, it's a deliberate action on my part that I acknowledge to the tenant.

In many instances, making yourself "whole" with each minor exchange allows a better chance for a deal that feels fair at the end. Sometimes, inexperienced negotiators concede multiple points and fail to receive anything in return. They may believe that they are storing goodwill and expect the prospect to compromise on subsequent or multiple issues. Later, when a larger capitulation doesn't happen—even if one party has granted many prior concessions—disappointment and bitterness can ensue. Perhaps it's human nature, but the memory of a conceded point can fade quickly. To prevent this, barter issues along the way, or specify that you are compromising now in exchange for future considerations.

SPLIT THE DIFFERENCE

There's a real estate adage that advises, "He who names a number first, loses." When two parties reach a stalemate on price, the sides will often offer to split the difference.

With that in mind, remember to leave yourself some margin. Most brokers and business people expect to negotiate a bit, so naming your bottom-line number out of the starting gate—despite your straightforward intentions—can seem inflexible and lead to an impasse.

I knew a no-nonsense asset manager who would become frustrated during lease renewals because tenants would expect to negotiate the proposed rental rate. Meanwhile, the asset manager had offered her bottom line (or close to it). Where's the fun in that? Whether she disliked negotiating rent or believed others would appreciate her directness, she boxed herself into a corner with little margin for negotiation. I learned that it's a good idea to understand the culture of the marketplace. If others expect to debate terms, then leave some wiggle room.

DON'T SPLIT THE DIFFERENCE

Parties can also make gains by focusing on the goals of each side, including the valuable noneconomic terms that play a role in any deal. For example, tenants may pay higher rent if they can obtain monument signage outside the building (assuming they're renting ample square footage). That's why it's important to understand what items are priorities for your tenants, and yourself.

REQUIRE A COUNTEROFFER

Oftentimes, prospective tenants or brokers will tell us that an economic or other lease point is unsatisfactory, without

> **Once It's Settled, Move On**
>
> Sometimes the prospective tenant will reopen an economic point of discussion. It is important to say, "That's a business point we've already agreed on." Otherwise, it's hard to conclude the deal and you end up compromising twice over a single issue.

offering a solution. Assuming you have already submitted a proposal, the tenant should respond. Take turns! If a prospective tenant complains the rent is too high but offers nothing more, seek a specific counteroffer. Some leasing personnel say exactly that; "I can't negotiate against myself. I look forward to your response."

LEAVE SOMETHING ON THE TABLE

While getting something for what you give works, other times you may choose to leave something on the table. That is, you don't drive as tough a bargain as you could have, with the goal of fostering goodwill. By being generous, landlords do their best to avoid festering resentments that can poison long-term relationships. With this approach, landlords may unbalance the quid pro quo just a bit, to leave tenants feeling satisfied that they negotiated a good deal. Some leasing professionals like to conclude negotiations with a concession at the close, which also helps them move on to the final phase: lease documentation.

CHAPTER 10

Understand Lease Clauses

"The devil is in the details."
—*American proverb*

GOAL: UNDERSTAND THE INTENT OF IMPORTANT LEASE CLAUSES AND TYPICAL LANDLORD AND TENANT CONCERNS IN ORDER TO CONSUMMATE A LEASE CONTRACT

Disclaimer: The legal language used in this chapter is intended for reference only and you should confer with your own attorney for legal advice on contracts and language.

Wait a minute, don't the legal gurus negotiate leases? Well, yes, although the process can become a little murky. It depends on whether the agreement is an amendment or a full-blown lease, and how amenable the tenant is to signing the landlord's lease form. Oftentimes, leasing personnel negotiate the bulk of the lease terms because if they are working from the landlord's standard lease form and the changes are nominal, the legal language has already been crafted. When faced with an impasse or with technical legal issues, though, real estate personnel usually engage counsel. In any event, real estate professionals strive to learn about lease clauses and their significance in order to better their leasing results. To that end, this chapter focuses on some important lease clauses, explains the intent behind them, and notes the objections that tenants sometimes raise in response to such provisions.

I knew an executive who needed to let go of one of his two leasing managers. Both had represented the landlord in substantial deals. The executive combed through the respective leases completed by the project managers. On the surface, the economic terms of the various deals appeared similar. By digging deeper into the leases, however, it became apparent that one manager had negotiated like a tenacious bulldog, conceding limited rights and crafting tight language (with legal help). The second project manager had been much less parsimonious—giving away extension rights, extra parking, monument signage, and so on. In down markets, landlords and tenants experience hardships that test the fine points and details of these lease clauses. Guess which manager kept his job?

Nolo (www.nolo.com)

A useful website dedicated to helping the layperson understand legal clauses.

Clauses That Contain Financial Terms

SECURITY DEPOSITS

Most leases call for a security deposit, often in the amount of one month's rent, from the tenant upon lease execution. Why have security deposits, especially when the tenant is creditworthy (as all your tenants should be)? Simply said, a security deposit motivates both the landlord and the tenant to get around the table to solve any problems that arise. All is well when the tenant and landlord enjoy a shiny new relationship, but should the dialogue crumble, a deposit provides an incentive to solve issues. Further, a security deposit may be the only no-risk, self-help remedy the landlord has under the lease. Last, by requiring a security deposit, the landlord retains a certain amount of leverage both during the lease term and after the term expiration with regard to the surrender of the premises. The security deposit encourages a tenant who is leaving to depart in a timely manner, with the premises intact.

> **A security deposit motivates both the landlord and the tenant to get around the table to solve any problems that arise.**

Common Objections and Concerns

Tenants will sometimes say, "We are a creditworthy company that pays our rent on time. Why do you need a deposit?" Regardless of the financial strength of the company—although that most certainly can affect the amount of the security deposit—most leasing personnel explain that deposits provide motivation to solve any (unlikely) disagreements. A response might be along the lines of, "We want to make sure that we all have an incentive to get around the table and resolve any issues."

LATE CHARGES AND INTEREST

This clause encourages prompt tenant rent payments by assessing late charges and interest if rent is not paid on time. The two methods—late charges and interest—address slightly different concerns. Late-charge penalties discourage the tenant from paying late every month, even though the tenant may eventually bring the account current. Interest charges, however, discourage a tenant from maintaining outstanding debt over longer periods of time.

Common Objections and Responses

Tenants sometimes ask for a grace period before interest or late charges start to accrue, and/or a lower interest rate or late charge. Some tenants will argue that they need protection against administrative mistakes, mail delays, and so on.

Many landlords try to avoid giving tenants a grace period because it takes away their incentive to pay rent promptly. After all, if tenants say their businesses are so disorganized that they cannot ensure timely rent payments, what does that say about their credit? In this situation, the landlord can explain that utility bills and other operational expenses need to be paid and that that requires timely rent payments. With respect to interest, the rate must be high enough that throughout the term of the lease, it remains a deterrent to late payments.

I found the clause on late fees and interest a pretty easy one to negotiate. If a tenant asked me to change this language, I would respond, "Let me get this straight, you mean you don't intend to pay rent on time?" It's tough to have a good response to that question.

OPERATING EXPENSES AND TAXES

This section addresses the definition of operating costs and taxes, the calculation thereof, and the payment process. Office leases usually fall in the category of full-service leases, meaning that the landlord pays for the costs associated with running the building and looks to the tenant to pay a pro rata share of increases in such expenses.

Tenants commonly negotiate this section, and it can be difficult because some issues may be business (i.e., financial) concerns, while other objections relate to the clause's language. Depending on the building, some tenants pay their share of increases in operating costs and taxes over a base amount that is expressed in dollars per rentable square foot, while in other buildings tenants pay their share of increases over the actual operating costs and taxes for the base year. (And still other leases are structured so that tenants pay their own operating expenses.) Note that operating costs and taxes are often defined and calculated separately so that, for example, a reassessment of the building that results in a reduction of taxes below the base level does not offset increases in operating costs. In other buildings, though, operating costs and taxes are bundled together for determining the tenant's share, so you need to know the policy for your building. Also, note that the tenant's share of increases in operating costs and taxes is calculated on the basis of the operating costs and taxes that would be incurred if the building were 100 percent occupied, even if the occupancy rate is lower. The rationale for this, which often has to be explained to tenants, is that absent such a provision, the landlord will end up paying a portion of the operating costs and taxes that are more properly attributed to the tenant's space.

When operating-cost savings are passed directly or indirectly back to the tenants, the tenants can be rewarded for choosing a sustainable building. Some landlords add green or other capital improvements to their buildings by incorporating lease language that allows owners to pass through amortized capital expenditures intended to reduce operating costs or improve the utility, efficiency, or capacity of any building system.

Common Objections and Concerns

While tenants negotiate many facets of operating expenses and taxes, the most common request is that the operating costs be capped at a certain increase per year. In addition, tenants will often want to negotiate various aspects of operating expenses, usually ones that have the ability to be large-ticket items: roof membrane replacements, Americans with Disabilities Act compliance, improvements intended to make a building more efficient, and so on. Landlords typically address these issues one by one,

A Yen for Legalese?

Commercial Lease Law Insider (commercialleaselawinsider.com) is penned for managers, owners, attorneys, and leasing professionals. This excellent newsletter explains lease clauses and solutions using real-life examples. Paid subscription and free e-alert both available.

and if not capping expenses, they may make modifications to individual line items. With respect to capital costs required to meet government regulations, often landlords explain that these costs are typically beyond the landlord's control and that such improvements are not necessarily adding value to the building (for the landlord's benefit), but are simply code compliance.

Clauses About Building Systems and Integrity

The next set of clauses deals with language intended to protect the landlord's real property, including the building systems such as HVAC, fire sprinklers, plumbing, and so on. Procedures regarding repairs, if needed, are also discussed. Although a tenant may not realize the benefit of these clauses, they serve to protect both the tenant and the landlord and ensure functioning building systems.

Who Says Latin Is a Dead Language?

ad valorem: "according to the value"
bona fide: "in good faith," implies sincere
good intentions regardless of the outcome
caveat emptor: "let the buyer beware"
de facto: "from the fact," common in practice, but not established by law
force majeure: OK, you're right, it's French,
not Latin, and it means a "superior or irresist-
ible force" or an event or effect that cannot
be reasonably anticipated or controlled (think
lightning, earthquakes, and hurricanes)
quid pro quo: "this for that" or "something
for something"
subrogate: from the Latin *subrogatus,* "to
elect as a substitute," to put something or
someone, such as a second creditor, in the
place of another with regard to a legal right
or claim

ALTERATIONS

Alterations, as opposed to tenant improvements, usually refer to construction or improvements *after* tenants have taken occupancy of the space.

The alterations clause protects landlords against liability for mechanic's liens, building code violations, uninsured contractors, code and environmental viola-tions, among others. Furthermore, certain alterations can adversely affect the structure of the building and/ or the performance of critical building systems such as

HVAC, electrical, plumbing, and other mechanical systems. Landlords are usually concerned with protecting the integrity of their building systems, which support a functioning, quality operation. As an example, if a tenant constructs a private office without the landlord's knowledge, the HVAC systems (and other electrical and fire systems) could be compromised. In addition to the potential for legal claims relative to construction, landlords are concerned with disruptions to other tenants.

Common Objections and Concerns

Tenants might say they do not want to seek the landlord's approval for every improvement they make and may cite an innocuous chore, such as painting the office kitchen. Some landlords approach this by asking the tenant to notify the landlord (in writing) of cosmetic improvements but then insist on approving more substantial improvements. Landlords explain that even something as simple as moving a wall can impact heating and air conditioning and fire sprinklers—systems involved in providing a safe and functional space.

Last, alterations clauses might contain a definition for a *trade fixture* as opposed to real property improvements. The clause sometimes makes tenants liable for any damage caused by the removal of a trade fixture. Occasionally an issue will arise as to whether a particular item that the tenant wants to install (such as customized, adjustable shelving) is a trade fixture that can be removed by the tenant or if it becomes part of the real property that reverts to the landlord at the lease end. This technical issue should be discussed with counsel.

DAMAGE AND DESTRUCTION

This clause typically addresses the procedure and time frames for repair in damage and destruction situations. Whether because of a localized issue (fire, for example) or an area-wide issue (an earthquake or hurricane, for instance), the clause outlines a process and the respective obligations of the landlord and tenant. The burden falls mostly on the landlord, even though the various scenarios are oftentimes caused by outside influences beyond the landlord's control.

Common Objections and Responses

This clause can be extremely difficult to negotiate because both parties have a risk of loss and impact to their respective businesses in a damage situation. Tenants are concerned about having their businesses closed and will want to know how long repairs will take, so they might object to the period of time allowed for reporting and making repairs. On the other hand, landlords must have rental income to pay their mortgages and other expenses. Accordingly, landlords need to know that they will have the opportunity to rebuild and restore their premises so that the leases remain in effect. Also, landlords may want the ability to terminate leases if they do not have significant funds to repair the damage or if repairs do not make economic sense.

Call me Debbie Downer, but lease negotiations involve imagining what bad things might happen (in order to protect your downside). I have found that explaining a scenario often helps tenants to understand the rationale behind requirements, time frames, and language. I might say, "Let's suppose an earthquake strikes. Many buildings are damaged. In a race to repair, dozens of owners submit permits for approval. The city inspector becomes overwhelmed, which lengthens the review process. So it may take us weeks to have a permit approved before we can pick up a hammer. Also, we'll be working with insurance companies and doing our best to accommodate tenants. Although conservative, that's why the process may extend to several months." A description of that sort helps clarify clauses that the tenant perceives as onerous. Because sometimes, what you imagine will go wrong, does.

Clauses About the Landlord's Control of the Property

The next set of clauses has to do with the ability for the landlord to maintain flexibility and control, primarily in terms of leasing. A lease creates an encumbrance—albeit one that the landlord is usually happy to have—with regard to space. There's a delicate line between providing tenants with support for their businesses and retaining the landlord's ability to maintain the building's value and operation.

USE

Use clauses deal with how the tenant uses the space, often drawing parameters about the type of business that may be conducted in the space. Leases contain this clause to ensure that the tenant does not use the premises for any purpose that is dangerous, poses issues for other tenants, threatens the integrity of the building or any of its systems, is illegal, and so on.

Common Objections and Responses

What response should you expect from the tenant on the use clause? Hopefully nothing. If a tenant resists this language, leasing personnel should look closely. What does the tenant have in mind? Any issue with this clause should prompt a heart-to-heart conversation between the landlord and tenant.

When tenants raise issues, you can find out what worries the tenants and address their specific concerns. As an example, commercial tenants may request a specific use such as storage or warehousing inventory.

> **What response should you expect from the tenant on the use clause? Hopefully nothing. If a tenant resists this language, leasing personnel should look closely. What does the tenant have in mind? Any issue with this clause should prompt a heart-to-heart conversation between the landlord and tenant.**

ASSIGNMENT AND SUBLETTING

This clause deals with the possibility of tenants subleasing their spaces or assigning their leases.

Common Objections and Concerns

Some tenants assume that so long as they pay rent, subleasing or assigning their lease doesn't have much impact on the landlord. As such, the tenant may have a difficult time understanding why a landlord wants to approve a subtenant or why the landlord should share in any subletting profits. Tenants are concerned about keeping the flexibility to sublease their spaces or assign their leases in the event they don't need (or can't afford) their leased spaces. As a practical matter, though, subleases can cannibalize a landlord's marketing efforts. For example, when tenants elect to assign or sublet their spaces, they may compete with the landlord for existing tenants that want to expand or prospective tenants who relish the lower sublease rate. By subleasing, tenants can undercut landlords' rental rates and force the landlords to charge lower rates than they would have otherwise. Then, landlords face the awkward situation of explaining to prospective tenants why they charge more rent for the same building and justifying how a direct lease is more beneficial than a third-party sublease.

In addition to blunting a landlord's competitive edge, sometimes a sublease assignment can leave the landlord with a financially unstable or less-than-desirable subtenant. While the tenant is still primarily responsible for the lease and rent, should the tenant default, the landlord could be looking to the subtenant to satisfy the lease obligations. What if the accounting firm you leased to decides to sublet to a start-up dog walking service? A proposed subtenant may impose on and excessively burden the building services or may not have a compatible use of the property. What if the law firm that rented the space subleases to a twenty-four-hour delivery company?

My tenant with sublease space used our proper-
ty's leasing flier with its pricey color photograph of
the building, bulleted list of amenities, and a floor
plan outline and map for its own sublease adver-
tisement. We'd created the full-color piece for our
direct space on our dime. Adding insult to injury,
the tenant's broker then called me a "turkey" in
front of my own tenant when I explained that our
marketing materials weren't to be used for others'
subleasing purposes. The last thing I wanted was to
compete with my own tenant. This uncomfortable
situation underscored the need to pay close atten-
tion to sublease language.

RELOCATION OF PREMISES

Relocation clauses allow landlords to move tenants
throughout the building (or project) from time to time
during the lease term, subject to some conditions for the
relocated space. At office parks with more than one building, a landlord might have the right to relocate tenants
to any of the buildings within the campus. The relocation right is important because of the leasing flexibility
it grants landlords, particularly when accommodating
tenant expansion or large prospective tenants.

Common Objections and Responses

Tenants want to eliminate this clause. They do not like the
unknowns of potential relocations, as moves are inconvenient and disruptive to business.

Many landlords try to negotiate concessions to this
clause rather than delete it entirely. But size matters. Large

tenants can be successful in having this clause deleted or significantly modified, because relocation can be cost prohibitive and physically implausible for them. Concessions to smaller tenants might include that the relocated premises are comparable to the existing suite in terms of distance from elevators, views, and so on, and some certainty that the tenant's rent will not increase (even in the event that the relocated premises are slightly larger).

SURRENDER AND HOLDOVER

The surrender and holdover clause deals with what happens in the event that a tenant does not leave the space in an orderly or timely manner. If tenants stay beyond their lease expiration date, the holdover rent might be twice as high as during the last month of the lease term. As a general rule, tenants control whether or not they will be in holdover status. They may have deferred their lease renewals, not calculated their move timing correctly, or simply failed to reach a decision with regard to their spaces. In these instances, landlords usually need all the leverage they can get to encourage tenants to reach a decision. Will they stay or will they go?

Holdover clauses can also hold tenants responsible for damages (like opportunity cost) resulting from not leaving the space; had the tenant vacated on time, the landlord may have been able to release the space. The holdover section can provide for the tenant to pay the landlord any lost rent, costs, or other lost profits caused by the tenant's staying in the space and hindering the landlord's ability to lease to a new tenant.

> ### Fair Enough
>
> When tenants complain that holdover rates are too high, the leasing representative often responds, "Of course the holdover rent is unreasonable—it is meant to be. We want you to make a decision."

Common Objections and Concerns

Tenants sometimes protest that "the holdover rate is prohibitively high." Tenants also try to eliminate the damages paragraph.

Of course the holdover rent is unreasonable—it is meant to be. Landlords set high holdover rates to encourage timely decisions with regard to space. In addition, holdover rates are artificially high because a landlord does not want the rate to be commensurate with the market rate at the time of lease expiration, as that would reduce the incentive for the tenant to make a decision. Landlords could potentially end up with month-to-month tenants and have their leasing hands tied, unable to make long-term commitments to anyone.

Lease Clauses: Extension Rights, Right of Offer, Right of Refusal, and Expansion Rights

The following section covers clauses that deal with tenant rights and space encumbrances. Generally speaking, these rights benefit the tenant and limit the landlord's flexibility with regard to leasing space. When negotiating a lease, a five- or seven-year term can seem an eternity. That longish horizon can lead negotiators to grant such rights to tenants, leaving the administrative burden for another day (or individual). Leasing agents and landlords, however, often come to rue these clauses because a complicated web of rights and encumbrances can so burden a space that it becomes challenging to lease. As such, many landlords learn to grant these rights judiciously.

To a large degree, rights are a function of the market at lease signature. In soft markets, landlords are often forced to grant a myriad of rights to a tenant, simply because competitors do. In tight markets, landlords can be stringent. Regardless, paying attention to the details, even when rights are granted, can make a difference to the landlord.

A word to the wise: understand and confirm all the existing rights of current tenants before discussing lease rights with a prospective tenant. Many landlords, property managers, and leasing professionals rely on software with color-coded floor plans and rent rolls to illustrate existing rights. Because new rights will be subordinate to existing rights, landlords need to be sure they have offered space in the appropriate priority and under the prescribed terms.

> **Generally speaking, these rights benefit the tenant and limit the landlord's flexibility with regard to leasing space.**

EXTENSION RIGHTS

This clause grants the tenant a unilateral right to extend its lease term, usually with written notice to the landlord. Oftentimes, the rent for the extension term is set at fair market value (FMV) at the time of the extension, meaning the typical market rent for similarly sized spaces, buildings, and amenities. The notice period can range between three and eighteen months and is usually a function of the square footage leased. Larger tenants have a longer notice date, presumably because a bigger space takes longer to rent, complete tenant improvements for, and so on.

Common Objections and Concerns

Tenants generally try to negotiate a percentage, such as 90 percent (or 95 percent) of FMV. Tenants argue that they are a known, rent-paying quantity to the landlord and, as such, should enjoy a rent discount. Second, tenants ask that notice periods be shortened.

Landlords oftentimes agree to 95 percent of FMV because they do indeed bear fewer expenses and uncertainties with an existing tenant than a new tenant.

Some landlords consider the notice period the most significant aspect of this clause. Consider a 10,000 square foot tenant with only a three-month notice period. It generally takes a landlord a certain amount of time to clean the space, place it on the market, tour prospective tenants, negotiate a lease, and construct tenant improvements. Depending on the market conditions, a larger space might take quite a while to lease. Landlords often make the notice period consistent with the time anticipated to market the space.

RIGHT OF OFFER

A right of first (or second or third) offer clause gives tenants first (or second or third) dibs on the right to lease a specific space. The landlord provides written notice of available space, at the same rent and on the same terms that the landlord intends to offer other prospective tenants. The tenant usually has a specified number of business days to accept the offer, after which the landlord can offer the space to other prospects. The clause usually requires the landlord to reoffer the space to the tenant in the event the landlord proposes to lease the space at an effective rent less than a certain percentage (e.g., 90%) of the rent or upon other terms which are substantially more favorable to another prospect.

Common Objections and Concerns

Tenants sometimes lobby to exercise their offer at a percentage of the rental rate that will be offered to other prospective tenants, arguing that they are a known quantity. Tenants also try to obtain longer response times, in order to give themselves maximum flexibility.

Landlords will sometimes accommodate a slight rent discount or modify the time frame required to respond to the offer.

When weighing rent versus response time, you need to ensure that you stay nimble in the marketplace. Response times of three to five days are often deemed appropriate, especially because the tenant, as an existing occupant, knows the property.

RIGHT OF REFUSAL

A right of first refusal is similar to the right of offer discussed above, but it assumes that the landlord has procured a viable prospect for the available space (as opposed to offering the space to the existing tenant without another interested prospect . . . hence the difference between *offer* and *refusal*). This type of clause is even more burdensome to landlords than a right of offer clause because they need to market the space, reach an approximate agreement on business terms, and then tell their prospects to wait while the existing tenants who enjoy a right of (first) refusal clause decide if they will take the space on the same terms. Whew! That's complicated.

Further, if the existing tenant declines and the landlord and prospect move ahead on the lease negotiation, the lease terms must usually be within certain parameters or the landlord will be forced to reoffer the space to the existing tenant. It is exhausting work for the leasing agent. Once you recognize this scenario, you will be reluctant to offer tenants a right of refusal clause. Instead, if you give away a right, it will be a right of (first or second) offer. Thus, the semantics of a right (*offer* vs. *refusal*) can significantly alter your leasing obligations and flexibility.

Common Objections and Concerns

Generally, tenants express similar objections as those under the right of offer clause (see above).

EXPANSION RIGHTS

This clause gives the tenant the right to expand into a specific space by giving written notice to the landlord by a prescribed date. The option's timing and available space are generally associated with another tenant's lease expiration, subject to any other rights on the space. Again, this type of right is restrictive because when (and if) the space becomes available, the landlord is obligated to lease the space within certain parameters. Many times the rent mirrors the rental rate under the tenant's existing lease.

Common Objections and Concerns

Tenants may try to get a discount on the rent for the expansion space. Also, tenants may try to obtain the shortest possible notice period for exercising their option. Many landlords try to keep the notice date as early as possible and the rent close to or at fair market value, or they try to avoid giving this right altogether. Landlords will sometimes talk about the benefits of having a great working relationship rather than a right on a specific space that may or may not suit the tenant in the future.

When I give a property overview at the start of a tour, I say, "We pride ourselves on long-term, quality relationships. Your company's growth is the type of problem we love to have! For example, our tenant XYZ initially leased 5,000 square feet of space, grew to 10,000 square feet, and now we're proud to have them as our anchor tenant with 30,000 square feet in Building B." I emphasize that we will do our best to accommodate the company's growth via ongoing dialogue and a strong relationship.

Lease Signatures and Delivery

Once lease clauses have been discussed and agreed upon, there's the logistical process of distributing the lease for signature, arranging its full execution, and delivering it.

LEASE FORMS

Landlords usually present their own lease forms for tenants to sign. Lease document lengths can vary dramatically depending on the size of the tenant, the length of the lease term, and even the quality of the space leased. Some examples include:

Fast Track Lease Forms

Many landlords employ fast track lease documents, a simplified or abbreviated version of the standard lease. Particularly well suited for a small or short-term lease, these documents allow for quicker negotiation because of their brevity. A pleasure to use, fast track leases streamline the process for all involved.

Similarly, lease renewals can be a short addendum to the existing lease, modifying the financial terms and updating only those paragraphs in the lease that are outdated or which both parties wish to change.

Tenant Lease Forms

Conversely, national (or international) companies with significant square footage and multiple locations often develop their own lease forms. These companies try to insist on signing their own form rather than the landlord's lease. Obviously, this type of arrangement favors the tenant and may require a significant time investment on the landlord's part to reconcile the property's standard lease with the tenant's form and ensure all the salient points are addressed. The question of whether or not to use a tenant's form depends on how intractable the prospective tenant remains regarding this issue and how badly the landlord wants the company as a tenant.

I once leased a 50,000 square foot office to an insurance company. At the tenant's demand, and because of its size and creditworthiness, we allowed the tenant to use its own lease form. It became critical to understand the tenant lease form because it would lack the nuanced advantages contained in our own lease document. My homework? To compare, clause-by-clause, the tenant's lease form to ours. The silver lining? Once the lease was signed, its administration became easier because of my familiarity with every clause. Honorary law degree not included.

ROUTING THE LEASE FOR SIGNATURE

Standard lease packages include multiple copies of the lease, with each signature or initial area tagged for ease. The documents are usually signed first by the tenant and then go to landlord for signature and final distribution. Most leasing professionals place a summary and financial analysis atop the lease forms for internal company review. The summary outlines the tenant, its business, the financial lease terms, and the tenant's credit strength. By shepherding the documents through the signature process (and communicating along the way), you eliminate the potential of a lease sitting on someone's desk (or in email), lost in a paper (or electronic) pile.

Using Technology to Expedite the Process

Technology provides tools to assist you in the lease documentation process. For example, video conferencing calls shrink the distances between continents and time zones. And word processing tools with markup functions allow edited lease language to be underlined or colored, which makes reviewing changes more efficient. On a larger scale, web-based transaction management systems let brokers and clients collaborate online during the entire transaction process; a single log-in shows all the pending deals, action items, responsibilities, and time lines. These tools change transactions in a meaningful way by streamlining leasing tasks, especially administrative ones.

While technological iterations offer potential time savings, there is a tension between the learning curve of technology and the efficiencies realized. Lease transactions have a pace of their own, and unless the deal coincides with an adaptation of new technology (or already skilled users), leasing professionals often prefer to finish a deal using their current practices, leaving the learning curve of new technology for future deals. The underlying concern is that the longer a deal drags on, the less likely it is to be consummated.

To complicate matters, the real estate industry has traditionally been a slow adopter of technologies. In a sector that places high value on personal relationships and, to some extent, protects its competitive edge of relationships and information, technology can seem threatening. As such, it's important to adopt the local technological tools of your marketplace so you are on the same electronic page as other negotiating parties.

SIGNED, SEALED, AND DELIVERED

Leasing is for the superstitious . . . or just plain paranoid. I've seen deals unravel over an innocent remark that led to unintended consequences. I once overheard two airline passengers discussing a nearly complete office lease. By the time we'd crossed a time zone, one passenger had referred the other to his best friend's brother-in-law, a broker. Hmmm, I wondered how this deal might change once others became involved. For that reason, I've learned to stay mum until the deal is closed. And I mean a lease that is completely signed, sealed, and delivered.

So you're almost at the finish line. Once the tenant signs multiple copies of the lease, the landlord does the same. The landlord distributes the fully executed lease or lease amendment to the tenant, landlord, and, if applicable, any other building ownership entity. The landlord banks the security deposit, the architect and contractor are notified to start the tenant improvement process, the landlord submits the brokerage commission invoice for payment, and it's full steam ahead.

Now the work of constructing the space and cultivating happy tenant relationships begins. In the meantime, utilize the good skills you've developed by leasing a space successfully, and your tenants should remain with you for the long term.

GLOSSARY

Some commonly used real estate
terms and their definitions.[1]

BOMA measurement: A standard for measurement as established by the Building Owners and Managers Association (BOMA) with its published *"Standard Method of Floor Measurement for Office Buildings,* an accepted and approved methodology by the American National Standards Institute (ANSI). Throughout the years the standard has been revised to reflect the changing needs of the real estate market and the evolution of office building design."

construction documents: The multipage, detailed set of architectural drawings that are prepared for permitting and used to construct space.

comparable: Used to discuss lease deals that can be considered worthy of comparison and/or of equivalent quality.

common areas: Areas of the building that are used by all tenants and their guests. Examples include the building lobby, hallways, bathrooms, fitness centers, etc.

elevation view: A frontal view, as if you are standing on the ground looking at an object in front of you.

encumbered space: "A block of space offered for lease by a landlord to which another tenant has some right to lease or occupy at some future date."

floor plate: "The gross square footage of each floor in a multistory building. Individual floor plate sizes may vary according to the design of a building."

gross lease: "A legally binding contract in which a landlord receives stipulated rent from a tenant and is obligated to pay all or most of the property's operating expenses and real estate taxes."

letter of intent (LOI): "A letter of intent is an agreement(s) between two or more parties before an actual agreement, such as a lease, is finalized . . . While LOIs may not be binding, provisions of them can be, e.g., non-disclosure and exclusivity."

load factor: "The load factor is calculated by dividing the rentable building area (RBA) by the usable area." (Synonym: add-on factor, the percentage of the common area attributed to each tenant's suite to calculate the rentable square footage.)

net lease: "A lease in which the tenant pays a share of operating expenses in addition to the stipulated rent. Disclosure of the specific expenses to be paid directly by the tenant is required."

partition: A wall which usually stops at the ceiling level.

personal property: Movable property, not permanently affixed to land or buildings.

plan view: A bird's-eye view, the perspective from looking down at a space.

real property: All structures (also called improvements or fixtures) integrated with or affixed to the land and/or building.

rentable square footage: A method of calculating floor area in office buildings that involves combining the usable square footage of a building with the common areas of the building (usually expressed as a percentage share per tenant) to arrive at the total rentable square footage, often per the method established by BOMA.

slab to slab: A fire-rated wall, built from the floor to the underside of the next floor.

space plan: A schematic or rough drawing by architects or designers to sketch the layout of an office space.

tenant improvements: Fixed (i.e., attached) construction improvements made to an office space.

turnkey: A complete product or service that is ready for immediate use; in real estate, it refers to a finished suite, ready for occupancy.

usable square footage: A method of calculating the square footage in tenant spaces that accounts for the area that can be used, but excludes common area measurements. The method for measurement typically refers to BOMA standards.

APPENDIX A

Market Research

Resources for market research (type *market* and/or *research report* into the search fields):

CBRE Group; www.cbre.us
Colliers International; www2.colliers.com
Cushman & Wakefield; www.cushmanwakefield.com
Jones Lang LaSalle; www.jll.com
Marcus & Millichap; www.marcusmillichap.com
National Association of Realtors; www.nar.realtor
National Real Estate Investor; www.nreionline.com
Newmark Knight Frank; www.ngkf.com
Subscriptions and/or databases for market research:
CoStar; www.costar.com
LoopNet (owned by CoStar Group); www.loopnet.com
Accruent; www.accruent.com
42Floors; www.42floors.com

APPENDIX B

Space Planning Indemnification Letter

Disclaimer: The legal language used in this letter is intended for reference only and you should confer with your own attorney for legal advice.

Dear Mr. Prospective Tenant,

It is the intent of [TENANT NAME] to occupy its premises at [BUILDING NAME AND ADDRESS] by the anticipated suite improvement completion date of [Month/Day/Year]. Upon execution of this letter, [TENANT] ("Tenant") agrees to indemnify [LANDLORD] ("Landlord") for the cost of space planning up to an amount not to exceed [$DOLLAR AMOUNT] in the event that Tenant does not consummate a lease with Landlord at [BUILDING NAME AND ADDRESS] by [Month/Day/Year].

Upon receipt of this executed letter at my office, I will authorize [ARCHITECT'S NAME] to commence space planning.

Sincerely,

[LEASING CONTACT]

AGREED TO AND ACCEPTED BY:

NAME: _____

TITLE: _____

APPENDIX C

Lease Proposal for a New Tenant

Here's the big, bold disclaimer: Every property has its own proposal, and your attorneys should review and approve your particular proposal, but for discussion purposes, a generic format is shown below. As a note, the name Main Street Office Center and any other sample names are fictional and intended for illustration purposes only.

Proposal to lease office space at 123 Main Street

Dear Prospective Tenant:

[Brief introduction, something like: We are pleased to present the following proposal to lease office space to your fine company . . .]

Main Street Office Center
Main Street Office Center has emerged as one of the premier office environments in the ABC area. Developed by

a partnership of Big Insurance Company and the principals of XYZ Development Company, 123 Main Street has the distinct advantage of being in an almost completely self-contained development. The Park features over one million square feet of first-class office buildings, an array of restaurant facilities, a high-quality hotel, and several freestanding financial institutions, all of which are combined into a richly landscaped, campus-like environment.

XYZ, the manager of The Park, currently manages in excess of five million square feet of office space in the Bay Area and maintains the services of full-time, on-site property management and maintenance staff at Main Street Office Center. XYZ takes pride in its ability to attract major national firms to its high-quality office developments. Main Street Office Center has attracted such diverse corporate headquarters as [name one, two, or three prominent companies if you have any headquartered at your space]; in the roster of regional offices are included such firms as [name your most prominent tenants—especially those that are representative of the prospective firm].

Location
As shown on the enclosed site plan, Main Street Office Center is located at the confluence of Interstate Highways 1 and 2, and it is within a half mile of US Highway 123. Main Street Office Center provides easy access to any point in the Big City area and has unparalleled access to Big City International Airport, which is less than three minutes away.

Main Street Office Center is serviced by three separate metro lines connecting Main Street Office Center with the Big City Transit Station. Main Street Office Center's excellent connections will only become more convenient in the future as additional stations are added to connect [name any transportation improvements under construction].

Amenities

The Park features several delightful eateries including ABC Deli, ABC Restaurant, and 123 Restaurant with indoor and patio seating, and several other choices in the nearby Convenient Shopping Center.

The Relaxing Hotel provides The Park with superior on-site lodging at an affordable price. The hotel features its own complimentary airport shuttle, meeting facilities, a spa, and a beautifully landscaped courtyard and an enclosed swimming pool. Your business associates will appreciate the convenience of the hotel's close proximity to your Main Street Office Center offices.

The Park also includes a myriad of support facilities including banks, savings and loans institutions, and convenient neighborhood services in the adjacent Convenient Shopping Center.

Finally, a completely equipped fitness center with lockers, sauna, and shower is located in The Park for tenants who enjoy the relaxing benefits of daily workouts.

123 Main Street—The Building

123 Main, a first-quality office building completed in late 2000, is composed of approximately 200,000 square feet on four levels, including 4,000 square feet of outdoor terraces overlooking The Park's park-like setting. Its impressive two-story lobby/atrium features elegant finishes, which include Brazilian cherrywood floors accented with rich granite, etched glass, and a John Doe bronze sculpture. Computerized building systems provide extremely cost-efficient operating and enhance a tenant's individual safety and comfort.

Initial Premises

The leased premises for Tenant will be approximately ___ rentable square feet consisting of Suite 456 ("Premises"). The subject area is highlighted on the enclosed floor plans.
Note: Some landlords also specify usable square footage, but because rent and operating expenses are all based on rentable square footage, this proposal states only the rentable square footage.

Expansion Option

Note: This is not a standard proposal item since it's a landlord concession. Sample language is included here, but many landlords do not offer this in standard proposals.

Tenant will be granted an option to lease _____ ("Expansion Premises"). Tenant must notify Landlord in writing of its election to exercise its option with respect to the Expansion Premises no later than _____ (___) months prior to the date of the lease expiration.

Right of Offer Space

Note: This is not a standard proposal item since it's a landlord concession. Sample language is included here, but most landlords do not offer this in standard proposals.

We will offer Tenant the following one-time right of offer, as indicated on the attached floor plan:
Right of [first, second, etc.] offer: Suite _____, approximately ___ rentable square feet.

Lease Term

The initial lease term shall be _____. Tenant will have ___ (___) (___) year options to extend the lease. Tenant must notify Landlord in writing of its election to extend the lease no later than ___ (___) months prior to the expiration of the initial lease term.

If Tenant exercises its Expansion Option with respect to the ___square foot expansion space, then it will be deemed to have exercised its option to extend the lease for the first ___ (__) year extension term.

Cancellation Right

Note: Again, not a standard proposal concession.

Tenant will have a one-time cancellation right at the start of the ___ year of the lease term, with ___ months prior written notice. The fee for the exercise of the cancellation right will be the sum of the principal amount of the unamortized leasing costs, including tenant improvements, space planning, lease commissions (including lease commissions to XYZ Management Company) and an additional sum which shall represent the non-discounted difference between the average rent over the term of the lease and the rent actually paid during the first ___ years of the lease term. We will calculate the actual fee based on a straight-line depreciation at __ percent annual interest, and will note such fee in the lease. The cancellation fee will be paid upon notice of the exercise of the right to cancel. The cancellation right shall be null and void if Tenant is in default of any term or provision of the lease from the notice date through the __ anniversary of the lease if Tenant relocates within a ten-mile radius of Main Street Office Center for reasons other than expansion, and assuming Main Street Office Center cannot offer Tenant expansion space.

Occupancy

The Premises can be made available for occupancy as early as [month/date/year].

Base Rent

The fully serviced rental rates per rentable square foot for the Premises, including both the Premises and any Expansion Premises then occupied, including a base amount for operating expenses and real estate taxes, shall be as follows:

Year(s)	Monthly Rental Rate
1	$X
2	$X
3...	$X...
11–15	Fair Market Rental Rates

In no case will the rent be less than the rent for the immediately preceding period.

Base Operating Expenses and Real Estate Taxes

A base amount for operating expenses and real estate taxes is included in the rental rates indicated above. Tenant shall pay its pro rata share of all operating expenses and real estate taxes in excess of the ___ calendar Base Year, excluding nonrecurring expenses* (including its pro rata share of any increased real estate taxes resulting from the project's sales or change in ownership during the lease term). Operating costs and real estate taxes for any year during which the average occupancy of the building is less than 100% shall be calculated based on the costs that would have been incurred if the building were 100% occupied.

*Alternative language: Tenant shall pay the stipulated base amount of $__ per rentable square foot per year, excluding nonrecurring expenses.

Storage Space

There is currently approximately ___ square feet of storage space available in the basement of _____. This storage space is accessible directly from the building's parking area via on-grade double doors or it can be accessible from the building's elevators. The current rental rate for storage space is $___ per square foot per month.

Tenant Improvements

We will provide Tenant with an allowance of $___ per rentable square foot for tenant improvements for both the Premises and any Expansion Premises.

Space Planning and Design

We will pay for the space planning and design costs associated with the preparation of one space plan, one minor revision, and one set of working drawings, assuming a fully executed lease. Subject to our prior approval, if Tenant wishes to employ its own space planner/architect, we will reimburse up to $___ per square foot of their fees.

Security Deposit

A security deposit in the amount of one month's rent shall be due upon lease execution.

Parking

We will provide Tenant with free on-grade parking adjacent to Main Street Office Center in the amount of one parking space for every 300 square feet of rentable office space leased.

Signage

We will provide Tenant with the opportunity to have a monument type signage in a prominent location adjacent to ___. The cost of the sign will be the responsibility of Tenant, and the location and design will be subject to approval of the City of _____ and Landlord. Tenant, at its own cost, will also be entitled to standard building directory and suite signage.

Security System

Security for buildings in Main Street Office Center is achieved with a Schlage system of dead-bolt locks on all tenant suites. Tenants will be provided with keys that will allow them entry to the building and their tenant suites after building hours and on weekends. In addition, a private security company periodically patrols the Premises and checks building entries on nights and weekends.

Building and HVAC Hours

The building's hours of operation are 8:00 a.m. to 6:00 p.m., Monday through Friday, excluding holidays. After-hours usage would be charged on an hourly basis. The current after-hours HVAC usage rate is $__ per hour.

Brokerage Commissions

Tenant represents and warrants that it has not been represented by a real estate broker who would be entitled to a commission in this Lease transaction (other than____). Landlord and Tenant shall hold each other harmless against the claims of any other broker or finder. [Landlord/Tenant] is responsible for paying the commission due ____.

Existing Lease Obligations

Landlord is unable to assume Tenant's existing lease obligations.

Contingency

This proposal represents a preliminary outline of proposed business terms, and both parties understand and agree that no binding contract shall exist until Lease Agreement has been fully executed by Landlord and Tenant. This proposal is subject to prior lease of all or any portion of the Premises. This proposal shall also be contingent on review and approval of Tenant's financials.

We look forward to your careful consideration and response to our proposal. We are available at any time to meet with you to discuss this proposal. We genuinely desire to structure a long-term, mutually beneficial transaction with Tenant's fine firm. If you have any questions, please call me at (###) ###-####. The terms of this proposal are valid for the next ___ days.

Sincerely,

[Name]

Leasing Agent

cc: [appropriate ccs]

AGREED TO AND ACCEPTED BY:

[Company name]

By: _____

Name: _____

Title: _____

A note on signature blocks: confirm that the signature block matches the entity for the financials you have reviewed and approved.

APPENDIX D

Proposal for an Existing Tenant

When we enter into discussion with existing tenants for renewal (extension) or expansion, there's an underlying lease already in place. Thus, any change to the terms becomes an amendment, usually a page or two long. The short form renewal proposal does not reiterate the amenities of the building because the tenant already knows them well. However, it's still good to tell tenants that they are valued and that you look forward to continued strong relationships.

The following sample language (and again, review your language with your attorney!) is intentionally brief in order to highlight business points.

Date
Prospective Tenant
Company Name
1234 Any Street
City, State, Zip

RE: Proposal to Lease Office Space
123 Main Street

Dear [tenant's first name],

[Landlord name] on behalf of [owner name] is pleased to present [tenant company name] with the following proposal to lease space at:

Premises: Approximately 5,000 rentable square feet, located on the fourth floor of the building.

Lease term/commencement: The lease term shall be five (5) years, commencing on January 1, 2012.

Annual, Fully Serviced Base Rental Rate:

Year 1: $___ per rentable square foot
Years 2–5: $___ per rentable square foot

Tenant Improvement Allowance: Landlord will contribute up to a maximum of ___ dollars ($X) per rentable square foot toward the cost of designing and constructing alterations within the Premises. Landlord's general contractor will construct the alterations. Landlord shall pay for the cost of one (1) preliminary space plan and one (1) revision. Any additional planning and construction related costs shall be paid by the tenant.

Operating Expenses/Real Estate Taxes: Tenant's base year and tax year shall remain ____.

Financials: Tenant shall provide Main Street Office Center with audited financial statements for the previous three (3) calendar years for Main Street Office Center's review and approval.

Security Deposit: The security deposit on hand shall be adequate to fulfill this requirement subject to review and approval of Tenant's financial statements.

Brokerage Commission: See prior proposal language. Alternate language: Landlord will offer a consultant fee of $___ per rentable square foot that Tenant may utilize to compensate its real estate consultant. However this consultant fee shall be amortized over the term of the lease at an interest rate of ___%.

Contingency: This proposal represents a preliminary outline of proposed business terms, and both parties understand and agree that no binding contract shall exist until a lease agreement has been fully executed by [landlord name] and [tenant name]. This proposal shall not be considered a reservation of the Premises and is subject to prior leasing of all or any portion of the Premises.

[Tenant's first name], we look forward to finalizing this lease renewal with you. Please call me at your earliest convenience to discuss this proposal. Should you have any questions please call me at (XXX) XXX-XXXX.

Very truly yours,
[Name]
Leasing Professional
Accepted & Agreed
Name _____
Title _____
Date _____

ABOUT THE AUTHOR

Alice Devine has over twenty-five years of commercial real estate experience. As a director of leasing for William Wilson & Associates (now EQ Office), Alice was responsible for leasing a multi-million square foot portfolio of Class A office space in the San Francisco Bay Area. She also created and taught a company-wide program focused on leasing and tenant retention. Earlier, at Norris, Beggs & Simpson, Alice was responsible for leasing and managing a medical and office portfolio.

Alice holds a Bachelor of Arts in economics from the University of California, Berkeley and has earned the Real Property Administrator and Certified Property Manager designations from the Building Owners and Managers Institute and the Institute of Real Estate Management, respectively. She is a former board member and active volunteer at the non-profit Rebuilding Together, which renovates homes and community centers.

www.devinerealestateguide.com

ACKNOWLEDGMENTS

Many thanks to John Hamilton, principal of Embarcadero Capital Partners, for teaching me how to lease to and retain quality tenants, challenging me in the best of ways, and offering office space in which to work. To Jill Benitez, Jim Arce, Carol Castro, Veronica Scharton, Carol Knorp, and Kim Russell, who offered feedback and added their real estate expertise. To Dave Tuck, authors Bruce Henderson and Anne Janzer, Lynn Everett and Holly Brady for edits, publishing guidance, and good humor. To Jan Travis for the start. To Annie Barnett and Halkin Mason, photographers extraordinaire. Thank you also to the editors and designers at Girl Friday Productions including Alexander Rigby, Valerie Paquin, and Christina Henry de Tessan for getting it right. And, of course, to the home team, for your support.

In addition to individuals, several organizations served as valuable resources, including the Fisher Center for Real Estate and Urban Economics at U.C. Berkeley, Stanford's Professionals in Real Estate, the Institute of Real Estate Management, and the Building Owners and Managers Association.

NOTES

Chapter 1

1. Connie Bruck, "Rough Rider," The New Yorker, November 12, 2007, accessed November 30, 2018, https://www.newyorker.com/magazine/2007/11/12/rough-rider.

2. Henry A. Crumpton, "Training," in *The Art of Intelligence: Lessons from a Life in the CIA's Clandestine Service* (New York: Penguin Group, 2012), 32.

3. "Research Reports," National Association of Realtors, accessed March 18, 2018, www.nar.realtor/research.

4. Richard J. Herring and Susan M. Wachter, *Real Estate Booms and Banking Busts—An International Perspective*, Group of Thirty, 1999, page 6, accessed March 28, 2017, http://www.group30.org.

5. Christopher Lee, "Real Estate Cycles: They Exist . . . and are Predictable," *Center for Real Estate* 5, no. 2 (Spring 2011): 7, accessed March 28, 2017, https://www.pdx.edu.

6. Ian Ippolito, "Should I Invest in Residential or Commercial Real Estate? (Part 2: Commercial)," The Real-Estate Crowd Funding Review, last modified January 15, 2016, https://www.therealestatecrowdfundingreview.com/residential-or-commerical---part-2.

7. Sue Shellenbarger, "How Saying Thanks Can Help Your Career," *Wall Street Journal*, November 21, 2012, D3.

8. Marcia Bell, "More than a Law Library: A Center for Justice," San Francisco Law Library, last modified Fall 2003, accessed March 28, 2018, http://www.sflawlibrary.org.

Chapter 2

1. Roger Staubach, "Leading the Way," interview by Scott Murray and Angel Carlton, Leading the Way, podcast, March 2, 2018, http://www.i4cp.com.

2. Ron Leuty, "Visa Moving Headquarters from San Francisco to Foster City," *San Francisco Business Times*, September 13, 2013.

3. Thomas A. Stewart and Sandra Kirsch, "BRAINPOWER Intellectual Capital is Becoming Corporate America's Most Valuable Asset and Can Be its Sharpest Competitive Weapon," Fortune, June 3, 1991, 44, http://www.fortune.com.

4. Matt Woolsey, "In Depth: America's Top 25 Towns to Live Well," *Forbes*, May 4, 2009, https://www.forbes.com/2009/05/04/towns-cities-real-estate-lifestyle-real-estate-top-towns_slide_17.html.

5. Adam Smiley Poswolsky, "What Millennial Employees Really Want," *Fast Company*, June 4, 2015, https://www.fastcompany.com/3046989/what-millennial-employees-really-want.

6. Norm G. Miller, PhD, and Dave Pogue, Do Green Buildings Make Dollars and Sense?, September 15, 2009, http://www.catcher.sandiego.edu/items/business.

7. Energy Star, backed by the US Government, in partnership with the Environmental Protection Agency, "2018 Energy

Star Top Cities," Energy Star, accessed April 18, 2018, https://www.energystar.gov/buildings/topcities.

8. Energy Star, backed by the US Government, in partnership with the Environmental Protection Agency, "2018 Energy," Energy Star, https://www.energystar.gov/about/federal_tax_credits

9. Jongmin Kim, Nathan Novemsky, and Ravi Dhar, "Adding Small Differences Can Increase Similarity and Choice," 225-229, December 20, 2012, http://journals.sagepub.com/doi/pdf/10.1177/0956797612457388.

Chapter 3

1. Marylin Bender, "High Finance Makes a Bid for Art," New York Times, February 3, 1985, F26, https://www.nytimes.com/1985/02/03/business/high-finance-makes-a-bid-for-art.html.

2. *Official SFMOMA Construction Time-Lapse,* produced by EarthCam, EarthCam/YouTube, May 6, 2016, https://www.youtube.com/watch?v=vRGqYL0XGOA.

3. "Pantone Color Systems Explained," Pantone, accessed May 29, 2018, https://www.pantone.com/color-systems-intro.

4. Audrey Shi, "Here are the 5 Youngest CEOs of the Fortune 500," *Fortune,* June 14, 2016, http://fortune.com/2016/06/14/here-are-the-5-youngest-ceos-of-the-fortune-500/.

5. Jacob Cass, "What Makes a Good Logo?," *Just Creative* (blog), July 27, 2009, http://justcreative.com/2009/07/27/what-makes-a-good-logo/.

6. See note 5 above.

Chapter 4

1. William Wilson, III, "http://wilsonmeany.com/people/william-wilson/," Wilson Meany, accessed November 30, 2018, http://wilsonmeany.com.

2. Ken Auletta, *Googled: The End of the World as We Know It* (New York: Penguin Group, 2009), 13.

3. Paul J. Zak, "Vampire Wedding," in *The Moral Molecule: The Source of Love and Prosperity* (New York: Penguin Group, 2012), introduction, xii.

4. David Eiland (president and co-owner, Just for Fun) in interview by author, San Francisco, March 2009.

5. Emily Post, "Etiquette in Business and Politics," in *Etiquette in Society, in Business, in Politics, and at Home* (New York: Funk & Wagnalls, 1922), 532.

6. Moumita Das, "Millennial Spotlight: Connecting With the Most Powerful Consumer Generation," PPAI Media, April 28, 2017, http://pubs.ppai.org/ppb-magazine/millennial-spotlight-connecting-with-the-most-powerful-consumer-generation/.

Chapter 5

1. Barbara Corcoran, "http://www.oprah.com/money/how-to-sell-your-house-fast/all," Oprah, accessed November 30, 2018, http://www.oprah.com.

2. Malcolm Gladwell, *Blink: The Power of Thinking Without Thinking* (New York: Little, Brown and Company, 2005), 23.

3. Ed Yong, "Justice Is Served, but More So After Lunch: How Food-Breaks Sway the Decisions of Judges," *Not Exactly Rocket Science* (blog), Discover, April 11, 2011, http://blogs.discovermagazine.com.

4. Johnny Mercer and Harold Arlen, "Ac-Cen-Tchu-Ate the Positive," Library of Congress National Recording Registry, 2015, audiotape, recorded 1944.

5. Ken Auletta, *Googled: The End of the World as We Know It* (New York: Penguin Group, 2009), 13.

6. Tim Springer, "Office Finder," entry posted July 19, 2011, http://www.officefinder.com.

7. Kingsley Associates and BOMA International, "Experience Exchange Report," accessed April 23, 2018, http://www. boma.org/research/Pages/eer.aspx.

8. Wallace Earle Stegner, *Crossing to Safety* (New York: Modern Library, 2002), 18.

9. See note 8 above.

Chapter 6

1. Rob Walker, "The Guts of a New Machine," *New York Times*, November 30, 2003, https://www.nytimes. com/2003/11/30/magazine/the-guts-of-a-new-machine. html.

2. Ben Waber, Jennifer Magnolfi, and Greg Lindsay, "Workspaces That Move People," *Harvard Business Review*, October 2014, https://hbr.org/2014/10/ workspaces-that-move-people.

3. Gloria Mark, Daniela Gudith, and Ulrich Klocke, "The Cost of Interrupted Work: More Speed and Stress," page 4, January 2008, https://www.ics.uci.edu/~gmark/chi08-mark.pdf.

4. Jennifer Smith, "Law Firms Say Good-Bye Office, Hello Cubicle," *Wall Street Journal*, July 15, 2012, Law, https:// www.wsj.com/articles/SB100014240527023036128045775 28940291670100.

5. Mike Moran, interview by the author, Menlo Park, CA, June 27, 2013.

Chapter 7

1. William Wilson, III (founder, William Wilson & Associates) in interview by the author, San Mateo, CA, August 25, 1999.

2. "Protect Your Interests When Leasing to Foreign Tenant," *Commercial Lease Law Insider*, August 25, 2016, https://www.commercialleaselawinsider.com.

3. "The Difference Between an Audit Review and Compilation" Grassi & Co., last modified August 17, 2010, http://www.grassipas.com.

Chapter 8

1. Sherry Turkle, *Reclaiming Conversation: The Power of Talk in a Digital Age* (New York: Penguin Press, 2015), 25.

2. Randy Pausch and Jeffrey Zaslow, "The Happiest Place on Earth," in *The Last Lecture* (n.p.: Hodder & Stoughton, 2008), 51-52.

3. Stanford University, "The Resilience Project," Student Learning Connection, accessed June 23, 2018, https://learningconnection.stanford.edu/resilience-project.

Chapter 9

1. James Traub, "The Anti-Trump," The New York Times Magazine, December 20, 1998, [Page #], accessed November 30, 2018, https://www.nytimes.com/1998/12/20/magazine/the-anti-trump.html.

2. Roger Fisher, William Ury, and Bruce Patton, "Preface to the Third Edition," in *Getting to Yes*, 3rd ed. (New York: Penguin Books, 2011), xiii.

3. Alex Lickerman, MD, *The Undefeated Mind: On the Science of Constructing an Indestructible Self* (Deerfield Beach, FL: Health Communications, Inc., 2012), 88.

4. Susan Cain, *Quiet: The Power of Introverts in a World that Can't Stop Talking* (New York: Random House, 2012).

5. Gary Noesner, "Top Tips from FBI Negotiator on Crime and Business," interview by Josh Wolfe, *Forbes*, last modified August 29, 2013, https://www.forbes.com/sites/joshwolfe/2013/08/29/from-waco-to-wall-street-a-discussion-of-crime-and-business-with-the-fbis-former-chief-hostage-negotiator/#657a98f2b106.

6. See note 5 above.

7. Fisher, Ury, and Patton, "Invent Options for Mutual Gain," in *Getting to Yes*, 3rd ed. (New York: Penguin Books, 2011), 63.

8. Sue Shellenbarger, "Just Look Me in the Eye Already," *Work & Family* (blog), *Wall Street Journal*, May 28, 2013, http://www.wsj.com.

9. Fisher, Ury, and Patton, "Introduction," in *Getting to Yes*, 3rd ed. (New York: Penguin Books, 2011), xxviii.

10. See note 9 above.

11. Fisher, Ury, and Patton, "Don't Bargain Over Positions," in *Getting to Yes*, 3rd ed. (New York: Penguin Books, 2011), 11.

12. Daniel Goleman, "Anatomy of an Emotional Hijacking," in *Emotional Intelligence* (New York: Bantam Books, 1997), 13.

13. Gary Noesner, "Top Tips from FBI Negotiator on Crime and Business," interview by Josh Wolfe, *Forbes*, last modified August 29, 2013, https://www.forbes.com/sites/

joshwolfe/2013/08/29/from-waco-to-wall-street-a-discus-sion-of-crime-and-business-with-the-fbis-former-chief-hostage-negotiator/#657a98f2b106.

Glossary

1. Maria Sicola, Commercial Real Estate Terms and Definitions, March 2017, http://www.naiop.org/-/media/Research/Research/Research-Reports/Terms-and-Definitions/CRE-Terms-and-Definitions-2017.ashx; National Association of Realtors, "Glossary of Commercial Real Estate Terms," Realtors Commercial Alliance, accessed June 29, 2018, https://www.nar.realtor/ncommsrc.nsf/files/commercial%20real%20estate%20glossary.pdf/$file/commercial%20real%20estate%20glossary.pdf; BOMA International, "BOMA Floor Measurement Standards," Building Owners and Managers, accessed June 29, 2018, http://www.boma.org/standards/pages/default.aspx.

SELECTED BIBLIOGRAPHY

In addition to the citations listed in the endnotes, I conducted general research and drew inspiration from the following resources:

Goldsmith, Belinda. "Yahoo Memo Sparks Debate on Pros and Cons of Working at Home." Reuters (London, England), 2013, Technology. Accessed June 19, 2017. http://www.reuters.com/article/us-workplace-flexibility-idUSBRE91P0S720130226.

Hemmer, Andy. "Select a Broker As You Would Other Service Professionals." *San Jose and Silicon Valley Business Journal*, July 4, 1999. http://www.bizjournals.com/sanjose/stories/1999/07/05/focus9.html.

Hlinko, John. *Share, Retweet, Repeat: Get Your Message Read and Spread.* New York: Prentice Hall Press, 2012.

Kats, Greg, Leon Alevantis, Adam Berman, Evan Mills, and Jeff Perlman. "The Costs and Financial Benefits of Green Buildings." U.S. Green Building Council. October 2003. http://www.usgbc.org.

Mooney, Steven. *Real Estate Math Demystified*. New York: McGraw-Hill, 2007.

National Association of Realtors. "NAR Code of Ethics." Last modified January 1, 2017. http://www.nar.realtor.

Pattison, Kermit. "Worker Interrupted: The Cost of Task Switching." *Fast Company*, July 28, 2008. https://www.fastcompany.com/944128/worker-interrupted-cost-task-switching.

"Protect your Interests when Leasing to Foreign Tenant." Commercial Lease Law Insider, August 25, 2016. https://www.commercialleaselawinsider.com.

Putzier, Konrad. "CoStar's Crusade." The Real Deal. Last modified August 1, 2016. https://therealdeal.com/issues_articles/costars-crusade/.

Reed, James, and Paul G. Stoltz, M.D. *Put your Mindset to Work: The One Asset You Really Need to Win and Keep the Job You Love*. New York: Penguin Books, 2011.

Shellenbarger, Sue. "Just Look Me in the Eye Already." Work & Family (blog). *Wall Street Journal*, entry posted May 28, 2013. http://www.wsj.com.

Tracey, John A., and Tage Tracey. *How to Read a Financial Report.* 7th ed. New York: John Wiley & Sons, 2014.

United States Government, in partnership with the Environmental Protection Agency. "About ENERGY STAR for commercial and industrial buildings." Energy Star. Accessed April 19, 2018. https://www.energystar.gov/buildings/about-us.

United States Green Building Council. Accessed April 18, 2018. https://new.usgbc.org.

United States Green Building Council. "Leed is Green Building." Accessed April 19, 2018. https://new.usgbc.org/leed.

Made in the USA
Columbia, SC
04 March 2019